STEVE YOUNG

★

JERRY RICE

East End publishes many other sports books including:

BASKETBALL SUPERSTARS ALBUM 1996
MICHAEL JORDAN*MAGIC JOHNSON
ANFERNEE HARDAWAY*GRANT HILL
SHAQUILLE O'NEAL*LARRY JOHNSON
STEVE YOUNG*JERRY RICE
TROY AIKMAN*STEVE YOUNG
KEN GRIFFEY JR.*FRANK THOMAS
BARRY BONDS*ROBERTO ALOMAR
MARIO LEMIEUX
THE WORLD SERIES: THE GREAT CONTESTS
THE COMPLETE SUPER BOWL STORY, GAMES I-XXVIII
MICHAEL JORDAN
SHAQUILLE O'NEAL
WAYNE GRETZKY

For more information on how to order these books, as well as many other exciting sports books, see the back pages of this book.

STEVE YOUNG

★

JERRY RICE

RICHARD J. BRENNER

EAST END PUBLISHING, LTD.
SYOSSET, NY

To the memory of my mother, Betty Brenner, who brought music into my life and who taught me by her example to be gentle with people and to judge them by who they were as people without regard to skin color, nationality, or possible religious beliefs.

And with love, as always, for Halle and Jason, and to all the children in the world, may you always play in happiness.

I also want to thank Jim Wasserman for all his time, his patience, and most of all, his caring. And I also want to thank Jason Brenner for his work on the manuscript. And thanks too, to Carlos Velez, Andy Fink, and Christy Walters.

STEVE YOUNG*JERRY RICE
First Printing/ July 1995
ISBN 0-943403-34-0

The cover photos were supplied by SPORTSCHROME EAST/WEST. The photo of Steve Young was taken by Vincent Manniello. The photo of Jerry Rice was taken by Rich Kane.

Cover design by Jim Wasserman.

Copyright © 1995 by Richard J. Brenner - East End Publishing Ltd.

Library Systems and Services
Cataloging in Publication

Brenner, Richard J., 1941-
    Steve Young * Jerry Rice / Richard J.
Brenner.
        p. cm.

    Includes bibliographical references.
    ISBN 0-943403-34-0

    1. Young, Steve, 1961- 2. Rice, Jerry.
3. Football players--United States--
Biography. I. Title.

GV939.Y68B7 1995   796.332'092'2 B--dc20

Provided in cooperation with
Unique Books, Inc.

This book is published by East End Publishing, Ltd., 54 Alexander Drive, Syosset, NY 11791.

Mr. Brenner is also available to speak to student groups. For details contact East End Publishing, Ltd., 54 Alexander Drive, Syosset, NY 11791, (516) 364-6383.

Contents

STEVE YOUNG

1 Getting it Right

Jon Steven Young was born October 11, 1961, in Salt Lake City, Utah, and lived there until his family moved to the posh suburb of Greenwich, Connecticut, when he was six years old.

Steve showed that he had unusual strength and athleticism when he was still just a toddler. "He was particularly well coordinated," recalled his dad, LeGrande, who is called Grit by almost everyone—including his wife, Sherry. "One day while I was doing push-ups, Steve, who was only two-and-one-half years old, asked if he could try. I said sure and he got down and did ten of them. By the time he was three, he was dribbling a basketball and getting it right," added Steve's dad who, in 1959, before he was a corporate lawyer, set the single-season rushing record at Brigham Young University.

In fact, the entire Young family—which includes Steve's younger sister and three younger brothers—is filled with outstanding athletes. Their home life was so centered around athletic events that when Sherry Young was asked about how the family spent its time, she replied, "Mostly we go to games."

But life wasn't only fun and games for Steve. When he was nine years old he was regularly beaten up by a schoolyard bully, and he was always the last boy taken in the neighborhood football games. "Those were some of the toughest days of my life," recalled Steve.

Steve also had to learn another of life's hard lessons, that losing is just as much a part of playing as winning. "He was a sore loser as a kid," said Steve's mom. "If he lost, you couldn't talk to him for a day. He always blamed himself."

When Steve was nine, he also got to go to his first ball camp, where he met Mike Ornato. Ornato was the coach of the Greenwich High School football team, and he made an extra-large impression on Steve. "In my mind, there was the president

of the United States, my father, and the high school coach."
Right then Steve started dreaming that one day he would play
football at Greenwich High.

Although Steve's dad had been a football player, he never
pushed Steve to follow in his footsteps. "My dad always told me
not to play football if it wasn't fun. That's the most important
part when you're young. But he also told me to give it all I had
once I had decided to do it."

Steve had absolutely no trouble deciding that he wanted to
play football. But he did give a lot of thought to whether or not
he wanted to practice the Mormon religion, as his parents did. "I
had to decide early on what I believed in because I was living
something that was hard to live," said Steve, referring to the
Mormon strictures against cursing, smoking, and drinking.
Steve decided to join the church, even though it meant that he'd
be behaving differently than all of his friends. "Growing up in
Connecticut, I used to think there were only four Mormons in
the world—my parents, me and Brigham Young," said Steve, in
a smiling reference to the founder of the religion and Steve's
great-great-great-grandfather.

In high school, when Steve went out to parties with his
friends, some of them would drink beer. Steve, though, always
drank milk. "But my friends always respected me, and no
human being ever had more fun," said Steve, who always acted
as the designated driver.

Steve was a straight-A student in the classroom as well as a
three-sport star on the playing field. His talent and personality
commanded so much respect from his teammates and his
coaches at Greenwich High that he was elected captain of the
baseball, basketball, and football teams. In his senior year
Steve, who throws left-handed but bats right-handed, was the
school's top pitcher and a .600 hitter on the diamond, a 20-
points-per-game scorer on the basketball court, and an

All-County quarterback who led an undermanned team to the district championship game.

"He took a team of very average athletes to that game," said coach Ornato. "He was a tremendous athlete and he always had a great work ethic, too." The one thing that Steve didn't have was a strong arm. "He was an excellent runner, but he wasn't gifted with a naturally strong arm," added Ornato. "As a sophomore and junior, in fact, he had a less than average arm for a high school quarterback."

Of course, the run-oriented wishbone offense that Ornato coached wasn't the type of system designed to help a quarterback develop his arm. "I don't think we ever practiced throwing the ball in high school," said Steve. "We threw maybe 10 times a game. I was actually embarrassed to throw the ball in public. I didn't enjoy throwing because I wasn't very good at it. We had to throw out of a rollout, no dropbacks. That's hard to do even now. I always just ran the ball. Why embarrass yourself?"

Steve's lack of experience in passing a football became a problem when it was time to decide on a college. Although Steve's grades would have gained him admission to just about any school in the country, Steve wanted to attend a school that had a strong football program as well as academic opportunities.

But weak-armed quarterbacks don't set the hearts of college recruiters beating strongly. In fact, the only college that actively recruited Steve was North Carolina, and they didn't plan on playing him at quarterback. "Above all, we thought he was an outstanding athlete," said Jack Himebauch, who was UNC's recruiting director. "We recruited him as a quarterback, but we thought he'd end up as a running back. They were a wishbone team and Steve liked to call his own number. When he turned upfield, he usually made something good happen."

In the meantime, Steve got to meet LaVell Edwards, the head coach of Brigham Young University, when Edwards came east to give a talk. Steve must have done some pretty fancy talking himself, because Edwards invited him to come out to BYU for a recruiting visit. But the trip turned into a disappointment when an assistant coach told him, "The only chance you have of playing here is by becoming a defensive back."

2 Cougar Country

That warning almost pushed Steve into accepting the scholarship offer from UNC, but in the end he decided on BYU instead. "It had nothing to do with my family ties there. I mean, who really thinks about his great-great-great-grandfather?" said Steve, referring to Brigham Young. "And I wasn't around when my father played there. It was just a gut feeling that it would be the right place for me."

It must have seemed like a strange choice to everyone else, though. Steve had never impressed anyone with his throwing ability, and coach Edwards had installed an offensive system that was so heavily geared toward the passing game, that its initials could have been AIR BYU.

Since Edwards's arrival at the school in 1972 he had turned out a trio of top flight quarterbacks, all of whom had finished their college careers among the top ten rated passers in NCAA history. But the fourth in the Edwards assembly line and the best of the bunch was Jim McMahon, who would end his career as the number-one-rated college quarterback of all time.

When Steve arrived on the field for his first practice in the fall of 1980, he was listed as the team's eighth-string quarterback, the very end of a long line that stretched up to McMahon, who was in his junior year. The first thing that Steve did was walk up and introduce himself to quarterback coach Dick Scovil, who was conducting a passing drill with the other quarterbacks on the team. The second thing that Steve did was take a snap from the center, drop back, and then trip over his own feet and fall right down on his backside. "Everyone laughed. I was so embarrassed."

Since the coaching staff didn't have any time to waste on an eighth-stringer, Steve worked on his own and learned whatever he could from watching McMahon.

"I tried to pick up as much on my own as I could. Just the way McMahon would practice taking snaps without a center. When I did it, I would cheat a little and place my fingers in exactly the right grip on the ball so I wouldn't have to adjust it while I was dropping back. But I noticed that Jim didn't do that. He shifted the ball from his left hand to his right while he dropped back, just like he would have to do in a game. I thought, 'Why am I cheating myself?' After that I practiced better."

Nonetheless, in December, at the end of Steve's first season, he still hadn't climbed up the depth chart. Coach Edwards, acting on the advice of QB coach Scovil, told Steve that he wasn't a part of BYU's plans as a quarterback. "I think we have our quarterbacks for the future," said Edwards. "We need defensive backs. We'd like to move you to safety. You're too good an athlete to sit around."

The news hit Steve so hard that he called his parents and told them that he was dropping out of college and coming home. "But my dad told me that if I left school I couldn't live at home. 'There are no quitters living here,' Dad told me, and that settled that.

"Looking back, I think almost every freshman goes through a shock like I did. You go from being the big high school star to eighth-string, and it's a big disappointment. I just needed someone to tell me to keep going."

One month later Steve's football career, and most likely his entire life, changed direction when coach Scovil resigned and was replaced by a new QB coach, Ted Tollner. During his first day on the job Tollner watched the quarterbacks throwing, and then told Edwards that he thought Steve had the tools to become the team's future quarterback. Edwards checked out Steve the next day and came to the same exact conclusion.

"He was an eye-catcher with his foot speed and his quick release," recalled Tollner. "The only thing that did not grade at the top was his arm. He had good velocity, but not great velocity."

14

Tollner had given Steve the chance that he had been hoping for and working toward. "All I wanted was a shot. With Scovil, I wasn't even getting a look. I thought I could throw. I just wanted a chance to do it. If I didn't make it after that, I would have played defensive back, receiver, running back, wherever they needed me."

By the time Steve's sophomore season was set to begin, he had leapfrogged up the depth chart to No. 2, right behind McMahon. And when McMahon went down with a knee injury in the middle of the 1981 season, Steve stepped in and threw for over 300 yards while leading the Cougars to a 32–26 win over Western Athletic Conference (WAC)—rival Utah State. Steve, the first southpaw QB in BYU history, was back at the controls the following week. But this time his 21 completions weren't enough to stop the Cougars from avoiding a loss that ended their 17-game winning streak.

McMahon was back in action for the next game, and he played so well throughout the season that he finished third in the voting for the Heisman Trophy, which is given each year to the person who is selected as the best college football player. But during Steve's brief stint as a starter, he had shown that the string of super quarterbacks at BYU would remain unbroken. The torch had been passed.

When Steve stepped into the starter's role in the fall of 1982, he also stepped into a bright spotlight. Following in the footsteps of McMahon and the other Cougar quarterback stars, he created a lot of expectations. After the first few games there was some doubt as to whether Steve could deliver the goods. The second game of his junior season, in particular, turned into a nightmare when the Georgia Bulldogs picked off six of Steve's passes. The following week, in a game that marked the inauguration of the expansion of BYU's stadium from 35,000-person capacity to 66,000, the Cougars lost to the Air

Force—one of BYU's WAC rivals.

The back-to-back losses stung Steve and shook his confidence. "There were times that I questioned myself in those early days," acknowledged Steve. "But I convinced myself that a throwing football team will make mistakes, and that I had to keep plugging away."

Which is exactly what Steve did. And his positive thinking helped him steady down and lead the Cougars to seven straight conference wins, which earned them the WAC championship and an invitation to play Ohio State in the Holiday Bowl. And while the Buckeyes dropped a damper on BYU's festivities by putting an emphatic 47–17 end to the Cougars' winning streak, Steve still managed to throw for over 300 yards and wind up with 3,507 yards of total offense, the second highest in the nation for 1982 and the third highest single-season total in BYU history.

The total numbers showed 3,100 yards passing—including an NCAA record 22 straight pass completions over a two-game stretch—a 62.7 completion percentage and 18 scoring passes, as well as 407 yards and another 10 touchdowns rushing. That performance earned Steve WAC Offensive Player of the Year honors and the ringing endorsement of Gil Brandt, who was the top talent scout of the Dallas Cowboys. "He's the best they've ever had there. And he's the most accurate passer I've ever seen. Period. Young simply refuses to throw a bad pass."

Steve, however, was far from satisfied with his performance. "If I complete 20 of 23 passes, I remember the three," said Steve, a perfectionist by nature, and someone who perhaps dwells too much on the misses and doesn't take enough satisfaction from the hits.

As he was about to start his senior season, Steve also acknowledged, for the first time, just how burdened he had felt by picking up the quarterback reins at BYU. "I tried to tell people that there wasn't a lot of extra pressure on me, but let's face it, there obviously was. It's hard to go out there and play your best when you're constantly thinking about trying to be as good as the ones who had played there before you. I think I'll be a lot more comfortable this year."

Although it seemed unlikely that Steve could play at a higher level than he had achieved in the previous season, that's precisely what he did. Steve kicked off the 1983 schedule by passing for 351 yards and a single TD, while picking up another pair of scores and 113 yards on the ground. And even though the Cougars wound up on the short end of a 40–36 shootout, Baylor coach Grant Teaff had caught enough of Steve. "I rate Young as the best quarterback I've seen. He does it all. We just couldn't contain him. He's faster than a lot of halfbacks."

After that opening game loss, Steve led the Cougars to 11 straight wins, and continued to light up the scoreboard while picking up yardage at a record-setting pace. Over the course of the first three games of the winning streak Steve bombarded Bowling Green with five touchdown passes and two TD runs; threw for two scores and completed an NCAA-record 18 straight passes against the Air Force; and threw for another pair of scores in leading BYU over UCLA, 37–35.

The Bruins were so intent on stopping Steve's passing that they played seven men deep, allowing the BYU running game to ramble for 265 yards. "Young is the closest player we've seen since John Elway to being a great quarterback," said then UCLA coach Terry Donahue.

What helped to make Steve so outstanding was his enthusiasm for the game and his willingness to constantly work at improving his skills. "I love practice. I can't wait to go back out each day. It never gets monotonous. It's a constant challenge," said Steve. "I haven't got to the point where I think I'm pretty good and I don't have to work anymore. This game is fun and I intend to keep it that way. And as long as I work hard, I think my play will continue to improve."

Toward the end of Steve's spectacular senior season, people started talking about him in terms of the Heisman Trophy. And that talk grew into a roar after the eighth game of the season, when Steve passed for a pair of scores to set an NCAA record for most consecutive games throwing a touchdown pass (19). Then, with 11 clicks left on the clock, he scrambled in for the score that carried the Cougars to a thrilling 38–34 comeback win over Utah State.

Steve set 13 NCAA records, including highest percentage of passes completed in a season (71.39), most total yards gained per game in a season (395.1), and most passes completed in a season (306). He was also a consensus All-American pick, and wound up as the Heisman runner-up, behind Nebraska running back Mike Rozier. But lots of people, including BYU coach LaVell Edwards, weren't convinced that anyone was better than Steve. "He's as good a football player as you'll ever find," declared Edwards. "I think the amazing thing about Steve is that he has come farther quicker than anyone I've ever seen. He's one of the most dominating performers you'll ever see."

Gil Brandt, the Dallas Cowboys' superscout, rated Steve at the top of his list, too. "He has tremendous movement and a good, accurate arm. He's got good speed, and he carries that entire football team. He's better than any of the quarterbacks they've had at BYU, and he's the guy I'd like to have in Dallas."

When Steve was asked which pro team he'd like to play for, he just shrugged. "Whatever comes will come. I don't worry about it. I think about things like graduation and law school," said Steve, who was an Academic All-American and a National Football Hall of Fame Scholar-Athlete. "Those things I can control. But with the draft, you know, there isn't much choice. You get picked and you go play."

3 There Must Be Some Way Out Of Here

As it turned out, though, Steve did have a choice, because in 1984 an upstart operation, the United States Football League (USFL), was in existence and bidding against the NFL for select players such as Steve.

Steve reportedly had a four-year, $4-million offer on the table from the Cincinnati Bengals, the team with the top pick in the NFL's 1984 draft. He also had an offer that was somewhere in the stratosphere from the Los Angeles Express, one of the teams from the USFL.

While Steve weighed the offers and the opportunities, he was bombarded with phone calls from some very high-profile people who hoped to influence his decision. Donald Trump, one of the richest men in America and the owner of the USFL's New Jersey Generals, was one of the people who tried to persuade Steve to join the new league. Steve was also courted by Pete Rozelle, who was the commissioner of the NFL, and by Roger Staubach, a Hall of Famer who had been Steve's favorite player when "Roger the Dodger" was the scrambling signal caller for the Dallas Cowboys.

In the end, Steve decided to sign with the Express so that he could become an instant starter, rather than accept the offer from the Bengals—which would have, in all likelihood, turned Steve into a bench warmer for a couple of seasons. Steve was also attracted by LA's coaching staff, which included John Hadl, a former All-Pro quarterback, and Sid Gillman, who had long been considered one of the game's top offensive innovators. Steve thought that one way or the other, either through a merger of the two leagues or a collapse of the USFL, he would eventually wind up in the NFL. But he reasoned that he'd be a lot better prepared for that opportunity if he had the on-the-job training that he would receive with the Express rather than by serving as a backup for the Bengals.

In March of 1984, Steve was scheduled to fly to San Francisco, meet his agent, and sign a contract with William Olderburg, the 46-year-old owner of the Express.

But as soon as Steve stepped out of his 19-year-old Oldsmobile—the car that his teammates at BYU had dubbed "The Tuna Boat"—he seemed to step right into an episode of "The Twilight Zone."

After he had parked the jalopy in the airport parking lot in Provo, Steve was whisked away in Olderburg's private jet to San Francisco, where he was picked up by a chauffeur driving a Rolls Royce and then driven to a downtown office building which housed the headquarters of Investment Mortgage International, Inc., a multinational company that had been founded by Olderburg.

Steve and his agent, Lee Steinberg, thought they were going to Olderburg's plush office to merely put the finishing touches on a contract that had already been negotiated between LeGrande Young and Don Klosterman, the general manager of the Express. The meeting, though, grew tense and drew out into the early hours of the next morning as Steinberg, concerned about the staying power of the USFL, insisted that Olderburg guarantee a substantial portion of the contract with a large cash payment.

Olderburg, enraged at not getting his way, rolled up a large wad of bills and threw them at Steve and his agent, while he screamed, "Here's all the guarantees you'll need."

At one point, long after the sun had set over the Golden Gate Bridge, Olderburg grew so irritated that he walked over to Steve and jabbed a finger in his chest while telling Steve what he thought about his refusal to sign the contract exactly as Olderburg had drawn it up. "If you touch me one more time," growled Steve, "I'll deck you."

A few minutes later, Olderburg's security guards were escorting Steve and Lee Steinberg out of the office building and into a gray and misty San Francisco morning.

But eventually the deal did get done and Steve signed what was at that time by far the biggest contract in the history of team sports—a $40-million gusher that was scheduled to go on pumping money into Steve's bank account through the year 2027.

"I almost fainted that day. I really did," said Steve, who immediately endowed a $183,000 scholarship to BYU as a way of thanking the school for the education he had received and the opportunity that he had been given to showcase his skills on the gridiron. "I remember talking to a reporter from Channel 5 in Los Angeles, and I had to hold onto a rail. It was unbelievable."

Suddenly, Steve was identified in headlines all around the country as "The $40-Million Man." "I don't think Steve was prepared for it, and I don't know how I could have prepared him for it," said Steinberg. "It wasn't treated like a sports story. It was a major cultural phenomenon."

The amount of money was so staggering and the publicity so unrelenting—unflattering—that Steve went into a shell. He even thought about canceling the contract. "The money just overwhelmed him," said Steve's dad. "The money became his nemesis and he continued to live as though he didn't have it. He almost decided not to go to Los Angeles."

Steve finally did decide to report. But he got off to a slow start and missed the first six games of the 1984 season because the USFL played a spring schedule and Steve wanted to finish his classes and graduate on time. Steve did start 12 games, though, and under the circumstances turned in a decent rookie season along the way, he became the first player in pro football history to rush for 100 yards and pass for 300 yards in the same game.

The Express, though, quickly started running on a local track as

Olderburg's financial empire touched a third rail and went up in smoke. The following year, the franchise was in such sorry shape that the USFL had to step in and take over the team to meet its payroll. But the turmoil continued to take its toll, and the Express was evicted from its training camp center due to unpaid bills.

The last straw for Steve was the fiasco surrounding the 1985 season finale. The team, in full uniform, boarded a bus for a 45-minute ride to a junior college stadium for a game against the Arizona Wranglers. Halfway to the field, however, the driver pulled the bus over to the side of the road and announced that he was going to stay there until he was paid for the trip. Although some of the players were ready to sit out the game, they finally decided to pass around the hat and pay the driver with their own money.

Due to the franchise's dire financial straits, the team hadn't bothered to sign any replacements for players who had been injured late in the season. So at the start of the game, the Express was down to one healthy running back—Mel Gray, who has since gone on to become an All-Pro kick returner for the Detroit Lions. When Gray went down with an injury in the third quarter, Steve was suddenly pressed into service as the team's one and only running back. "It felt like a high school game out there," said Steve. "I was waiting for the cheerleaders to come running off the bus."

After two undistinguished seasons in a second-rate league, Steve wanted out so badly he paid more than a million dollars to get released from his contract. The USFL was in total disarray and about to sink into oblivion, and Steve was anxious to give his stalled career a jump-start. "You want to feel like you're going somewhere, accomplishing something," said Steve. "That's where it was really hard."

Unfortunately, life wasn't about to get better any time soon for Steve, because his NFL rights were at that time held by the

Tampa Bay Buccaneers, which was as low as you could go and still be in the NFL.

Steve, who signed a six-year, $5.4-million contract with the Bucs in the summer of 1985, wound up wasting two more years of his pro career. The Bucs, as usual, were a terrible team during Steve's term with them, managing to win only four of 32 games during the 1985–86 seasons. And while Steve's play didn't set the league on fire, it was hard to spark a team with such low morale. A lot of the players were just there to pick up their paychecks while they went sleepwalking through their assignments during games.

"One time we were playing the Bears, and one of our coaches looked me right in the eye and said, 'Look, Steve, I know everybody's sort of quit playing here, so don't expect to get a lot of protection. This is the kind of game where you could really get hurt. Be careful out there.' I couldn't believe it. How can you enter a game thinking like that?"

On that Tampa Bay team with Steve luckily was veteran Steve DeBerg, who had quarterbacked the Bill Walsh-coached San Francisco 49ers before he had been beaten out by Joe Montana. DeBerg realized that Steve, a diamond in the rough, required a master jeweler who could supply the polish that would allow the young quarterback's talent to shine through. "What Steve needed for his career to go to the next level was to be exposed to some top NFL coaching," said DeBerg. "I told him the perfect place for him was San Francisco, with Bill Walsh."

Confidentially, while DeBerg was advising Steve to find some way to get to San Francisco, Sid Gillman, who had been one of Steve's coaches with the Express, was singing his praises to Bill Walsh.

"He's the finest quarterback athlete I've ever seen," raved Gillman, who has seen all the great quarterbacks. "And he can throw any kind of pass that needs to be thrown. He can drill it in there, he can lay it in, he can touch it in—and on top of that he has tremendous intelligence."

Walsh took a close-up look at Steve and quickly saw the vast potential that had been covered up by the ineptness of the Bucs. "Tampa couldn't protect the passer, plus they were running a dated offense," declared Walsh. "So Steve looked bad there." Walsh realized that Steve could become a top flight quarterback if he was on a good team and received quality coaching, so Walsh executed a swap that brought Steve to the 49ers for the 1987 season.

4 Waiting in the Wings

Steve's arrival in San Francisco didn't set off any fireworks or bring him instant stardom. For one thing, he had to learn the 49ers' offensive system, a system that requires pinpoint passing and exquisite timing between the quarterback and his receivers. For another thing, Walsh had to perform a salvage job on Steve, who had spent the previous four years submerged in football oblivion.

"When he came to San Francisco, Steve was pretty shaken up in regard to his self-confidence and shaken up as to what he might be able to accomplish on a football field," recalled Walsh, who would eventually go on to become a TV analyst and then take over the coaching reigns at Stanford University. "Steve had spent a number of seasons just being totally frustrated and maligned."

Finally, the 49ers already had a starting quarterback, a fellow by the name of Joe Montana, who is widely considered to be the greatest signal caller ever to lace up a pair of cleats. Montana had already led the 49ers to two Super Bowl wins before Steve arrived in San Francisco, and he would lead them to two more over the next four years while Steve waited in the wings.

During the course of those four seasons as Montana's backup, Steve absorbed as much as he could by practicing diligently and watching Montana smoothly run one of the most efficient offensive machines ever assembled. And whenever Montana was injured—which wasn't often—Steve would step in and produce mostly spectacular results. In his limited playing time, which amounted to something less than a full-season spread over the four years, Steve wound up throwing for over 2,500 yards, including 23 touchdowns and only six interceptions, while contributing another 659 yards and four touchdowns on the ground. Truly spectacular numbers for a starter, let alone for a backup quarterback.

Steve had started to show that he could turn into something special during his first season in San Francisco, when he brought down the Bears with four touchdown passes. The following season, in a game against Minnesota, Steve put on another prime-time display, which included a 73-yard TD toss to wide receiver John Taylor and an almost unbelievable 49-yard broken field run that left a string of Viking defenders grasping for air and falling to the ground. The TD jaunt, with 1:58 left in the game, lifted the 49ers to a 24–21 win and helped earn Steve the NFC Offensive Player of the Week Award. The run was so astonishing that Steve Sabol, the president of NFL Films, called it, "The single best run in football over the last 25 years."

But those magical moments were spread too thinly over the four years that Steve played caddie to Montana. So by the end of the 1990 season, a season in which Steve sat and watched while a healthy Montana started all but one game, he was ready to consider leaving the 49ers and joining a team that needed a starting quarterback. "I just wanted to get on the field," said Steve as he recalled that frustrating time. "I just couldn't take it anymore."

It had been eight years since he had started out in pro ball and the sands of his football timer were starting to fill the bottom of the jar. The dilemma for Steve, though, was that he liked San Francisco and felt that the 49ers' offensive schemes were perfectly suited to his quarterbacking skills. So after a lot of soul-searching and discussions with his agent, Lee Steinberg, Steve decided to stay put for the time being. "My mission ever since I got here was to be ready to play spectacular football, not just substitute football," said Steve. "Part of the crazy drive about being here and not wanting to go elsewhere, even as Joe kept going and going, was that there is a benchmark of championships here that there is nowhere else. I just wanted to keep that tradition going. That would be the real test for me."

5 Nightmare

Steve finally got the chance to take the test when an injury to Montana's right elbow put Joe "Cool" on the shelf for the 1991 season. This was the opportunity that Steve had dreamed about for a long time, but it quickly turned into the most trying nightmare that he had ever experienced.

As soon as Montana's situation became public, it seemed as though the entire San Francisco Bay Area went into mourning. There was an unmistakable sense of loss, as if something precious and irreplaceable had been taken from them. And Montana's replacement became a convenient if irrational target for their terrible disappointment.

In a way, and up to a point, the reaction was understandable, even to Steve. Montana, with his four Super Bowl rings, had become bigger than life. It wasn't just the winning that elevated Montana to the level of a living legend. There was also his cool and elegant style, and his remarkable ability to bring the team from behind in the fourth quarter—and to do it more often than any other quarterback who had ever played the game.

Lost in the glitter of Montana's true greatness, though, were the seasons that he struggled, the games that the 49ers lost, and the times that Joe didn't get it done. It was as though everyone in San Francisco was living in a fairy-tale world in which time would always stand still and Montana would always be leading the 49ers to last-second victories and Super Bowl championships.

It's unlikely that anyone could have taken Montana's place and not been treated as an intruder in that world of make-believe. It might have helped, though, if Steve had gotten the 49ers off to a quick start. It also might have helped if Steve's frantic, scrambling style wasn't so different from the cool, patient approach that Montana had developed. And what might have helped most of all was if Montana had supported Steve instead of going out of his way to let everyone in the Bay Area know that he didn't consider Steve to be one of his best buddies. But none of that happened, and Steve didn't get a whole lot of help in struggling through that trying season.

Although Steve put up strong enough numbers to be named the NFL Offensive Player of the Month for October, the 49ers as a team weren't performing anywhere close to expectations. The year before, with Montana at the helm, the Niners had sailed to an NFL-best 14–2 record for the second consecutive season, and were on their way to their third straight Super Bowl appearance until a fourth-quarter fumble by running back Roger Craig in the NFC championship game gave the Giants a chance to kick a game-winning field goal with only 0:04 left on the clock. But through the first half of the 1991 season, those same 49ers were stalled at 4–4, and all the fingers were pointed at Steve. The media and the 49ers fans were hysterical and hypercritical, and even some of Steve's teammates blamed him for the team's fall from grace.

After one tough loss, the frustrations and whispered regrets about what would have been if only Montana was healthy surfaced with a vengeance. Linebacker Charles Haley, who was eventually traded to the Dallas Cowboys, went ballistic and blasted Steve in the 49ers' locker room. Then Jerry Rice, the 49ers All-Pro wide receiver, poured oil on the fire when he evaluated Steve by saying, "He's a great running quarterback." The implication, of course, was that Steve scrambled too often instead of sitting in the pocket and passing the ball, which was true. But saying it in public didn't do anything to boost Steve's confidence or to get the media and the fans off his back.

It would take time and experience before Steve would feel comfortable enough to realize that his over-reliance on his feet was upsetting the receivers and disrupting the carefully crafted offensive schemes. Through experience he would learn to stay in the pocket more and let the receivers finish running their routes. And he would also learn that when he scrambled he should keep his head up and his eyes downfield, looking to throw first and run only when none of his receivers were open.

But no one seemed to be willing to give Steve that time.

In the ninth game of the season, after throwing a team record 97-yard scoring strike to wide receiver John Taylor, Steve, went down and out with an injury to his left knee. Third-string quarterback Steve Bono then stepped in, and after losing one outing, led the 49ers to five straight wins. In the last two wins, Bono threw six touchdown passes while leading the Niners to Montana-like come-from-behind rallies, the first of which earned him NFC Offensive Player of the Week honors. Although Steve had been dressed and ready to play in those two games, George Seifert—who had replaced Walsh as head coach prior to the start of the 1989 season—kept him on the bench and let Bono play out his hot hand. It wasn't until Bono went out with a knee injury of his own in the third quarter of the following week, that Steve got back on the field. Steve finished out that win for Bono and then closed out the 1991 season by throwing three TD passes and running for a fourth as he led the Niners to a 52–14 bashing of the Bears.

Steve's hot finish allowed him to compile a league-high 101.8 QB rating. Only 12 other quarterbacks in the history of the NFL had ever topped the century mark, including, of course, Joe Montana, who had done it three times and who also owned the highest single-season rating, 112.4, as well as the all-time highest career rating.

Despite the uniqueness of Steve's personal accomplishment, the bottom line was that the 49ers, with a 10–6 record, had finished out of the playoff picture for the first time since 1982—and most of the blame was directed at Steve. Although 10–6 records are usually good enough for a team to make it into postseason play, Steve was more than willing to accept his fair share of the responsibility for the 49ers' unexpectedly early start into the offseason. "To be a great QB, your team must be great," said Steve. "That's what your job is." But it was unfair and inaccurate to lay all of the team's failure at Steve's feet. And the sad irony of Steve's statistical leadership was that in the eyes of most San Franciscans—including a majority of his teammates—Steve wasn't a leader at all and placed no better than third on the QB depth chart behind the still-injured Montana and Bono.

It wasn't only a question of not making the playoffs, though. There was also the fact that Steve hadn't demonstrated an ability to bring the team from behind as Montana had done with such breathtaking regularity, and as Bono had done twice in only six starts.

The critics also carped that Steve had scrambled too often, disrupting the team's finely tuned passing game and upsetting Jerry Rice, who was angry about not getting the ball delivered to him as well or as often as he would have liked—the way, it seemed, that Montana had always delivered it.

The irony of the situation was that Steve seemed to be one of the only people on the planet who remembered a time when the Candlestick Park crowd had been calling for Montana's head.

"I guess one of the best learning experiences I had was in 1987 when Minnesota beat us in the divisional playoff game. They benched Joe and people were booing him. *Booing Joe.* They started clamoring for this new guy, me, to be the quarterback. This is how they treated the guy who had taken them to two Super Bowls. I remember it so vividly. And it wasn't pretty."

6 It's My Job

During the offseason, when it appeared that Montana was headed for a complete recovery, and with Bono available as a more than capable backup, the 49ers' high command decided that Steve was expendable. "Remember where we were in March of 1992," said 49ers president Carmen Policy. "The coaches said that Joe was throwing better than he had in years. And the prospect of Steve Young being an unhappy camper would have been a distraction to the team."

Ultimately, no team came up with the players and draft choices that the 49ers considered to be fair compensation for Steve, although a trade with the Raiders involving wide receiver Tim Brown came tantalizingly close to being completed.

It turned out to be the best trade that the 49ers never made, because Montana's injury didn't heal in time for the 1992 season. After a spirited competition in the preseason games, Seifert named Steve as the team's opening-day starter.

Although Steve had gotten the nod from Seifert, most San Franciscans, as well as a majority of the 49ers, thought that Bono had outplayed Steve during the previous year and in the preseason games. But everyone was just hoping that Steve was only a temporary stand-in anyway, someone to hold down the fort until Montana could ride into action and lead the Niners' charge back to the top of the standings.

Steve's season got off to a shaky start when he suffered a concussion on the fifth play of the opening game. While his head was ringing like an unanswered telephone, Bono took over and calmly hit on two scoring passes that spearheaded the 49ers to a 31–14 win over the Giants. The following week, the Niners bowed to the Bills 34–31, despite a spectacular performance by Steve, who had returned to the lineup and who threw for a career-high 449 yards and three touchdowns.

Instead of concentrating on Steve's awesome accomplishments, however, Bay Area critics claimed that Montana would have found a way to win the game and not just put up big numbers. The following week, Steve threw for a pair of TDs and ran for a third in leading the Niners to a 31–14 win over the New York Jets. In the locker room, though, one reporter asked Steve if he felt responsible for the broken leg that John Taylor suffered when he had been hit while leaping for a high pass that Steve had thrown—as if Montana had thrown only perfect passes that receivers never had to jump or stretch to reach.

Even after Steve had led the 49ers on a five-game winning streak capped by a 56-point explosion against the Falcons and had been selected as the NFL's Offensive Player of the Month for October, the long shadow of Montana continued to hang over him. A chorus of critics, led by Jerry Rice, claimed that Steve wasn't throwing enough to Rice, Montana's favorite target—and arguably, the greatest receiver to ever catch a football.

Although Steve was upset and hurt by the unrelenting criticism, even in the face of a five-game winning streak, he reacted with astonishing poise and even put a positive spin on his predicament. "It's part of enjoying the process of life," claimed Steve. "It's not only about enjoying life when things go your way, but enjoying times when it's a little bit tougher."

The flu knocked Steve out of the next game, a loss to Phoenix which dropped the 49ers' record to 6–2 at the halfway point of the season. But Steve came back strong and KOd the Falcons once again by throwing for three TDs in a 41–3 rout at Atlanta. Falcons defensive end Tim Green was going to be sleeping a lot better knowing that Steve was headed out of town. "On Sunday morning when you have to play Young, you wake up with a sickening feeling and a headache. I can honestly say those are the only times I've ever approached a game conceding that an opposing player is going to make big plays no matter what we do."

The following week, Steve took a giant step toward winning the confidence of his teammates when he threw a pair of fourth-quarter TD passes that rallied the Niners to a 21–20 win over New Orleans and broke a first-place tie with the Saints. "Those last drives, he was just as calm as Joe ever was," said veteran guard Guy McIntyre.

Steve stayed so hot that he finished the season with a league-leading 107.0 quarterback rating—and became the first player in NFL history to lead the league in consecutive seasons with a quarterback rating over 100. Steve, who also led the league in touchdown passes and in completion percentage, capped his spectacular season by being named the NFL's MVP and the Player of the Year both by *Sports Illustrated* and *The Sporting News*. But of all the honors that Steve gathered, the one that meant the most was the Len Eshmont Award, which is voted on by the 49ers players and given to the player that they select as the most inspirational and courageous. "When you see what Steve's gone through and how he's hung in there when things didn't look real good, it says a lot for Steve's character," noted linebacker Michael Walter. And even Jerry Rice had climbed on Steve's bandwagon. "He's had an MVP year, no doubt about it. He has an attitude now, you can just look at him whenever he takes the field, he's got confidence in himself."

It had been a long time coming, but Steve had arrived where he wanted to be. "This is something I always knew I would do, once I had the opportunity to grow into the position."

Most importantly, Steve had piloted the 49ers to an NFL-best 14–2 record, including a season-ending 8–0 run that put them on a roll heading into the playoffs.

Steve's first postseason start came at home against Washington on a Candlestick Park field that had been turned into a semiswamp by a week of steady rain. Steve, though, overcame the slippery conditions and shot the Niners into a 17–3 halftime lead on a pair of scoring strikes—a five-yard toss to John Taylor and a 16-yard dart to tight-end Brent Jones. In the second half, however, a stalled offense and two fumbles by Steve allowed Washington to turn the fourth quarter into a 17–13 nailbiter.

Over on the sidelines, the 49ers' offense was in a state of disarray. "Everyone's yelling and screaming," related tackle Harris Barton. "Some guys are going over to Steve and saying, 'Hey, brother, let's get going.' Others are staying away from him. There's near-panic out there."

As Steve led the 49ers back onto the field, Montana, who had finally returned to action in the second half of the season's final game, took off his jacket and started warming up. "It was only a precautionary move," said Seifert afterward. "I thought Steve might have been banged up diving for that fumble on the previous possession."

Steve, though, was fine, as he demonstrated by taking the 49ers on a time-consuming drive and positioning the field goal that stretched the Niners' lead to 20–13, which is just how the game ended. Afterward, a lot of the San Francisco reporters seemed more interested in Steve's turnovers and the Montana angle than they did in Steve coming through with the win. But Steve wasn't interested. "The thing I'll focus on is the big drive and we'll just go on from there. I'm here now and it's my job."

Troy Aikman, the quarterback of the Dallas Cowboys team that the 49ers were about to meet in the NFC championship game, also thought that Steve had passed all the tests. "He earned the MVP award and he deserves to be playing," declared Troy. "He's handled the situation with Joe Montana in an admirable fashion, and I think he's answered all the critics."

What Steve couldn't quite answer, though, was the firepower of Aikman and his Cowboy teammates. Steve might have guessed that it wasn't his day when, on the third offensive play of the game, he connected with Rice on an apparent 63-yard touchdown pass, only to have it called back because of a holding call on Guy McIntyre. "It would have been a heck of a start," lamented Steve. "That one was tougher as the game wore on because we kept thinking about it."

Steve had the 49ers even at the half, 10–10, but Aikman put the Cowboys ahead for good with a third-quarter touchdown pass to Emmitt Smith. The 49ers did make a fourth-quarter run at the Cowboys as Steve directed a masterful 93-yard drive which he ended with a TD toss to Rice that cut the Dallas lead to 24–20 with 4:22 left in the game. The 49ers were hoping to shut down the Cowboys and get the ball back in Steve's hands. But Aikman shot those plans down with a four-play TD drive that salted the game away and made the final score 30–20.

The loss was very hard for Steve to accept. "It's tough to put into words. Here we really expected to go all the way this year. There aren't a lot of pats on the back at this point. Right now, it hurts." But after taking a little time to recover and to think about how far he'd come and how much he had accomplished, Steve couldn't help but smile. "Now, I can't wait, I just can't wait until next year.

7 Roller Coaster Ride

Steve's life in 1993 was like a year-long roller coaster ride, starting in the offseason when the 49ers' management couldn't seem to decide whether Steve, who had led the NFL in passing the previous two seasons, or Joe Montana, who had played one-half of one game in those two seasons, would go to training camp as the team's first-string quarterback. After a series of contradictory statements from George Seifert and Carmen Policy that made the Niners' management look inept, the situation was finally resolved when Montana was traded to the Kansas City Chiefs for a No. 1 draft pick.

While the three-ring circus was being played out in San Francisco, Steve was back at BYU, trying to concentrate on his last semester of law school classes. Although Steve was stung by the team's refusal to say that he was number one, despite his two passing titles and MVP award, he never took any slaps at the team's management or at Montana. "I understand how the organization was feeling. Here, after all, is a guy who has led them to four Super Bowl wins. It was a very emotional situation, and I think everybody tried to do the right thing.

"But when this is all over, I may be able to say that I had the strangest career in pro football history."

Once Steve arrived in training camp, he was way up after signing a five-year $26.75-million contract that made him the highest paid player in the NFL until Aikman signed an even bigger deal later in the year. But a few weeks later, he was down in the dumps after breaking a bone in his left thumb.

The thumb, which swelled to the size of a sausage, caused Steve to start the 1993 season in erratic fashion. Over the first four games, he threw eight interceptions, one more than he had thrown in all of 1993, and only six touchdown passes. Over the next seven games, with his thumb nearly healed, Steve was almost unstoppable as he threw for 16 TD's and only two INT's, while posting a QB rating of 122.7.

It was during that seven-game streak that Steve reached the zone that only the great quarterbacks ever attain. "The field seemed to open up and the players seemed to slow down. I knew where everybody was without looking, sometimes without even thinking about it."

Steve's teammates also noticed that he had taken his game to a higher level. "His recognition, his timing, his quick decisions remind you of Montana," said offensive tackle Steve Wallace. "He's no longer just a great athlete playing quarterback, he's a great quarterback in his own right."

Steve had also grown more mature and learned to accept the fact that miscues are an inevitable part of life. "You're going to make mistakes sometimes. You just can't get caught up in them." And he also grew a thicker skin so as to take the sting out of unjustified criticism. "You have to learn to ignore what people say when they don't know what they're talking about. You can't get upset about it."

Although Steve cooled down over the final five games of the regular season, he still finished with a 101.5 QB rating and became the only player to lead the NFL in passing and break the century mark in three successive seasons. Along the way, Steve completed a team-record 183 passing attempts without an interception, and became the first quarterback in 49ers history to throw for over 4,000 yards in a single season.

"He is the most effective quarterback playing the game today and my choice as the best simply because he's such a brilliant athlete," declared Bill Walsh, when asked to compare Steve and Troy Aikman. "Both are absolutely gifted athletes. Rarely are there more than one or two players like this at any one time." "They are it," added Fritz Schurmur, the defensive coordinator of the Phoenix Cardinals. "No question about it. How do you choose between them? They're either one and two, or two and one."

Although Steve appreciates what he's accomplished and the awards and the praise that he's earned, he never allows himself to be too content with where he is at. He always wants to be aiming himself at the next target. "Let's say I acknowledge it's a great feeling and then I push on, so that there's always an edge to things."

Although Steve had finished the 1993 season in a mini-slump and the Niners had dropped three of their last four games to finish at 10–6, they had won the NFC Western Division, and Steve wasn't about to allow the San Francisco media to downplay the team's chances in the playoffs. "I am not going to let myself or the rest of the team feel like we're in a jam. We've overcome mistakes all year long."

Then the Niners went out and backed up Steve's words by demolishing the Giants in a divisional playoff game—and they did it against one of the stingiest defenses in the NFL. Steve, who completed 17 of 22 passes for 226 yards, directed the 49ers to scoring drives on four of their first five possessions. Running back Ricky Watters, who rushed for five scores, set an NFL postseason record for touchdowns in a single game. "Our offensive line was awesome, I mean really awesome," said Steve with a happy grin. And the much maligned Niners defense, which had been ranked 28th in the league against the run, stuffed the Giants' number one rated running game.

But Steve and the Niners came crashing down to earth the following week as they were once again stampeded by the Cowboys in the NFC championship game, 38–21. "I'm trying to keep a stiff upper lip here," said Steve, who didn't take any consolation from his 27 completions or 287 passing yards that were accomplished despite a relentless Dallas defense that constantly kept their rush in Steve's face. "I never would have believed we'd come down here and get beat by this score. They did a great job. We have to earn the right to do this again."

When Steve was still playing for the Buccaneers, Sid Gillman had made a prediction. "Steve Young is a Super Bowl quarterback," declared Gillman. "I'd bet my life on it. Put him in a good organization that has a good passing concept and I promise you he'll take them to a Super Bowl."

8 Setting the Standard

No one could argue against the 49ers being a first class organization, but during the preceding few seasons their defensive unit hadn't been equal to the offensive unit or—even more importantly—the defensive unit of the Dallas Cowboys. And as Jerry Rice noted, the 49ers weren't going to get back to the Super Bowl without superior defense. "You win championships with defense, and that's something Steve hasn't had. You've got to have a great defense just like you have to have a great offense."

The 49ers management took the necessary steps towards rebuilding the defensive unit by working some salary cap magic and persuading a quality of group of free agents to bring their talents to San Francisco for the 1994 season. The principal additions were linebacker Ken Norton, who had been the heart and soul of Dallas's defense, and All-Pro cornerback Deion Sanders, the best pass defender in the NFL.

Despite the influx of defensive stalwarts, however, the 49ers still got off to a shaky start by losing two of their first five games, including a 24–14 loss to Joe Montana and the Kansas City Chiefs.

It was during the fifth game, a 40–8 pasting at the hands of the Philadelphia Eagles that the 49ers season and Steve's career may have reached a defining moment. Seeing that Steve was getting pounded into the Candlestick turf by a Philly defense that was blowing through an injury-riddled offensive line, coach Seifert decided to put up the white flag and pull Steve out of the game during a series in the third quarter. "It was just to protect him from the beating he was taking," explained Seifert.

Instead of expressing gratitude about being rescued from the beating he had been receiving, Steve flew into a rage and began berating Seifert for taking him out of the game. "I don't care how bad the situation is," he told Seifert, "I want to finish everything I start."

The sideline explosion by the usually soft spoken and mild-mannered quarterback seemed to galvanize his teammates. In some peculiar way, that outburst rallied the team behind Steve in a way that his excellent and courageous play never had.

"I think that game was the turning point for the team, for the organization, for the coaching staff and for Steve Young," said 49ers president Carman Policy. "With that eruption of emotions and passions he always kept beneath the surface, he suddenly got our attention."

"He became one of the guys," noted Seifert. And in doing that, Steve also became, for the first time, a team leader.

The following week Steve had to provide that team leadership on the field when the 49ers fell behind the Lions in Detroit, 14–0, and their season seemed to be slipping away. Guard Jesse Sapolu summed up their predicament perfectly. "Coming on the heels of the Eagles' debacle, the light at the end of the tunnel was getting pretty dim."

Steve, though, turned up the wattage by rallying the 49ers from that two touchdown deficit to a 27–21 victory over the Lions. That triumph was the spark for a ten-game winning streak, which didn't end until the season finale, when Steve and most of the other starters played only sparingly. The string of victories included a psychologically important 21–14 win over the Cowboys, a game in which Steve threw for two scores and ran for the third against the team that had become the Niners' nemesis.

Under Steve's leadership, the 49ers had taken great strides towards securing their chance of a Super Bowl championship since they had stumbled out of the starting gate at the beginning of the season.

"I look back on those early games and I'm very proud of what we did, because it was tough.", said Steve, "We came up with some victories when we could have seen our season slip away."

But instead of sliding down, the 49ers climbed to the top of the league's standings with a 13–3 record. The influx of defensive players had done their part, while the offensive unit was so explosive that the team scored 505 points, the fourth highest total in NFL history.

"This offense has the answers to anything that anyone can do defensively," said Steve with a sense of supreme confidence.

"Their offense is definitely awesome," agreed Giants coach Dan Reeves. "It's as good an offense as I've seen in a long time. And Steve Young is simply a magician with the ball."

But more important to Steve than the praise of outsiders, was the hard-fought battle for recognition that he won from his teammates, and especially from Jerry Rice—who until this season had never seemed entirely able to let go of the memory of Joe Montana.

"We've always had an offense that put points on the boards, but with this offense it's something different," noted Jerry. "I think it has something to do with Steve Young."

Steve had, produced a spectacular season, leading the league and setting team records for pass completion percentage (70.3), and TD tosses (35), while running for seven scores and compiling a 112.8 quarterback rating, which eclipsed the single-season record of 112.4 that had been established by Joe Montana in 1989.

"We couldn't function without Steve Young," said Deion Sanders, who was named the NFL's Defensive Player of the Year. "He's everything to this team."

The players and the coaches in the NFL showed that they agreed with Sanders by selecting Steve as the Sporting News Player of the Year. And the writers from the Associated Press made the decision unanimous when they choose Steve as the NFL's MVP, allowing him to join Montana and Hall of Famers Johnny Unitas and Jim Brown as the only two-time winners of the award.

"I don't think you can have a better season than Steve did," summed up coach Seifert.

There was no doubt that Steve, who had won his fourth consecutive passing title, was at the top of his game and generally considered to be the premier signal caller in the league. Steve had always had superior athletic skills, but with added experience he had learned how to better read defenses, and to exploit his talents to the team's maximum advantage. But the biggest area of growth of Steve, and the reason for his emergence as the game's best quarterback, was that he had finally gained the inner confidence that he needed to be able to assert himself in a positive way, and thereby establish himself as a leader of the San Francisco 49ers.

As tight end Brent Jones noted, "He's taken on a leadership role that he never had before. He definitely has earned the respect of the guys by his play and his toughness and his overall demeanor."

Steve, without bragging or any false modesty, also knew how far he had come. "I think I'm a lot better, I think I've just grown in leadership and preparation and reading defenses, everything. I said after the '92 season I had a lot of growing to do and a lot of maturing and a lot of improvement that was out there for me to go after. And I still feel that way. So, it's exciting for me to sit here and know there's more out there."

But no one knew better than Steve that he would never fulfill his own standards or the expectations of the team and its fans if he didn't lead the 49ers to a Super Bowl victory.

As his friend and agent Lee Steinberg noted on the eve of the playoffs, "There is no question that this is his last great challenge. He's been to the Pro Bowl. He's been MVP. He's won every statistical index. But the great challenge is to lead a team to victory in the Super Bowl. Ultimately, that's how legends are created in the NFL. So the bottom line is that his greatest test lies ahead."

Steve took the first step in that challenge by leading the 49ers to a 44–15 blowout of the Bears in a divisional playoff game. That win earned them their third consecutive NFC Championship Game matchup against the Dallas Cowboys, who had overcome a lot of obstacles to post a 12–4 record before powering their way past the Packers, 35–9, in their divisional playoff contest.

This was the game that teams and most NFL fans had been pointing to since the dog days of training camp. But this time Steve, who threw for a pair of TDs and ran for a third, was able to help the 49ers turn the tables on the two-time defending NFL champion by leading San Francisco to a 38–28 decision over Dallas. Although Steve didn't post great passing stats, he did team up with Rice for the play of the day on a 28-yard scoring strike with 0:08 seconds left in the first half that stretched the Niners' lead to 31–14. Then Steve wrapped up the Niners' scoring for the day with a three-yard run that gave them the cushion they needed to withstand a strong second-half rally by the Cowboys. That win over Dallas lifted a big load off Steve's shoulders, and put a big smile on his face as he looked forward to the trip to Miami and a meeting with the San Diego Chargers on Super Sunday.

"We're playing one more game, the Super Bowl," said Steve with uncharacteristic emotion. "It's what I've always wanted. It will be a special stage to showcase this team. We deserve it."

The 49ers, who had walloped the Chargers 38–15 in a regular season game, were the most overwhelming favorites in Super Bowl history. Steve, though, just seemed to thrive on the pressure of having to produce a win in the biggest game of his life.

"We've been the overdogs in a number of games this year. I know we're risking everything. And if we lose, it will be an absolute train wreck."

As it turned out, though, it was the 49ers who did all the wrecking, starting with the opening series of plays when Steve hit Jerry Rice with a 44-yard scoring strike at the 1:24 mark, the fastest score in Super Bowl history.

Steve also ignited the Niners on their very next possession with a 21-yard scramble, and then teamed up with Ricky Watters on a 51-yard pass and run touchdown that upped the 49ers' lead to 14–0 less than six minutes into the game.

Steve, who was throwing the ball with laser-like precision and running the offense with the mastery of a great maestro, threw two more first-half scoring strikes as the 49ers took a 28–10 half-time lead.

After a third-quarter TD gallop by Watters, Steve closed out his star-studded performance by throwing a pair of touchdown passes to Rice as the Niners coasted to a 49–26 rout of the Chargers.

Steve—whose six touchdown passes set a Super Bowl record, and who ran for a game-high 49 yards—was an overwhelming choice as the games MVP.

"Is this great or what?" bubbled Steve with a smile as wide as the Golden Gate Bridge. "I mean I haven't thrown six touchdown passes in a game in my entire life. Then I throw six in the Super Bowl. Unbelievable!"

Winning the championship also allowed Steve to finally, and perhaps, completely, step out from under the long shadow that Joe Montana's greatness and four Super Bowl rings had cast over his career.

Steve showed just how much the game and his performance meant to him when in the postgame locker room he hugged the Lombardi Trophy to his body as though someone was about to steal the Super Bowl victory away from him.

"No one, *no one,* can ever take this away from us. No one, ever. It's ours.

"There were times when this was hard," said Steve, looking

back at the long road that he had traveled to get to this moment. "Before, I was pressing too hard, trying to outdistance criticism and skepticism. But my secret to success in a way is that I have shown up for work every day no matter what was going on.

"It was difficult to face and some days I wasn't sure I was doing very well. You know the standards I had to live up to," said Steve, referring to the legacy that he had inherited from Joe Montana. "That's why this is one of the most precious times in life—to finally get there. This is the greatest feeling in the world.

"I grew and learned that you just have to get through the bad stuff. It wasn't fun then, but it sure is fun now! In the past, I might have looked to what's the next hurdle, whereas now, no one else defines it for me anymore. I feel like I've set my own standard and now, it doesn't matter what the game, what it is, there's a certain standard you play to. That's my hurdle."

In another corner of the 49ers' locker room, coach Seifert summed up the situation. "Joe Montana was phenomenal and established the standard. And Steve Young is talented enough and works hard enough so that he can maintain the standard. Whatever critics he may have had, the way he played, he has got to be one of the greatest quarterbacks of all time."

And according to Mike Shanahan, who is now the head coach of the Denver Broncos, but who was the 49ers' offensive coordinator from 1992-4, Steve's future is only going to get brighter.

"It takes a special guy to have the type of consistent success that Steve has had. I think over the next four or five years people will find out just what a great player Steve Young is."

But no matter what happens from here on out, Steve has already established himself as one of the top quarterbacks of all time, and he has the awards and statistics to prove it. In terms of career QB ratings, he ranks as the all-time leader at 96.8. And he is also the career leader in pass completion percentage at 63.2.

In both of those categories, Steve has taken over the number one spot from the now-retired Joe Montana. And while Steve is thoroughly devoted to football and bringing Super Bowl trophies home to San Francisco, there is a whole lot more to Steve's life than simply passing a ball down the field.

Steve, who spent a lot of his offseasons studying law at BYU, finally received his degree in 1994. At his graduation, he reacted with a mixture of seriousness and levity. "This has been a big goal for a lot of years. It hasn't been real easy. But I'm glad I'm educated to do the things I'd like to do. And now at least my dad thinks I'm qualified to do something, like get a real job."

Steve also figured that his law degree could come in handy against blitzing linebackers. "I'll sue for assault and battery on the field," joked Steve. "It won't just be 15 yards; it will be 15 yards and a cash settlement."

The real reason that Steve has worked so hard to become a lawyer, though, is that he has a deep and abiding interest in helping others. "People are in trouble," said Steve. "This huge, ugly system faces them and you're the only way to get people through the maze. If you're ethical and have a lot of care for individual people, you can help. I can help them through a system that is confusing even to me. We have to find a way to reach people, because it's easy to get lost."

Steve has always spent a lot of time and a lot of his money helping others. "The only fun I have with money is to be able to spread it around and do some fun things for people," said Steve, who lives very simply despite all the money that he's earned.

One example of Steve's helping others involved a Russian physicist who was teaching a summer course at BYU. Steve heard that the scientist had extremely bad teeth and was in constant pain, but couldn't afford to get them fixed. "Even the dentist said he'd never seen anything like it," said Steve, who took it upon himself to set up the appointment and pay the dental bill.

Steve is constantly committing random acts of kindness, like playing Santa Claus at a homeless shelter. While other people may look down their noses at people who have taken a fall, Steve realizes that most homeless people aren't lazy and didn't choose that way of life. He knows that those unfortunate people, at least for the time being, have been dealt a blow that's knocked them off their feet. "There's such a misconception about it, that people have done something wrong. But these people—especially the kids—have nowhere else to go," said Steve, with the clear understanding that bad times can happen to anyone.

Steve has also spent a lot of time helping Native Americans. "He goes down with me to the reservations to give seminars, helping kids with their self-esteem," related Dale Tingey, Director of American Indian Services in Provo. "He shares instances in his life when he's failed and they realize that if he can overcome it, they can, too. And he helps organize fund-raising dinners for scholarships that have sent hundreds of Indian students to college. He has a great love for the people."

In 1992, Steve set up his own charitable operation, called "Forever Young." The foundation is organized to fund charitable organizations that, "encourage the development, security, strength, and spiritual vitality of the family."

"To me, it's people getting along, doing the little things. It's basically the family and then your extended family, which really extends to anyone you come in contact with. That's what matters. You can't change the world, but you can change your little part of it."

Steve scrambles for some yardage while at BYU.
Courtesy BYU.

Perfect form!
Photographed by Michael Zagaris.

Steve sets up.
Photographed by Tony Inzerillo.

Steve looks for an open receiver.
SPORTSCHROME EAST/WEST. Rich Kane

Steve and Jerry embrace on the sidelines of Super Bowl XXIX.
Photographed by Michael Zagaris.

Jerry heads for the end zone.
Photographed by Michael Zagaris.

Jerry climbs a ladder against Cincinnati in Super Bowl XXIII.
Photographed by Michael Zagaris.

Jerry goes in for a score against Denver in Super Bowl XXIV.
Photographed by Michael Zagaris.

Jerry fights for extra yardage.
Photographed by Michael Zagaris.

Jerry and Steve on the interview stand after win in Super Bowl XXIX.
Photographed by Michael Zagaris.JERRY RICE

JERRY RICE

1 Catching Bricks

Jerry Rice was born on October 13, 1962, in Starkville, Mississippi, and raised 35 miles away in Crawford, a tiny spot of a town with about five-hundred residents. "Blink your eyes and you'll miss Crawford," notes Jerry.

Jerry's dad, Joe, was a bricklayer who worked long, hard hours under the hot Mississippi sun, but there was never enough money for Joe and his wife, Eddie, to stretch across the eight children in the Rice family.

"If we went on a school field trip," remembers Jerry, "the other kids could buy candy and Cokes and souvenirs and things. I couldn't. It was tough to deal with."

For fun, Jerry and his five brothers would chase the neighbors' horses who grazed on the Rice farmland. When the boys caught the horses, they would go galloping bareback across the field.

But most of the time when Jerry and his brothers were not attending school, they were out working with their father, earning needed dollars by helping him lay the bricks that went into a lot of the buildings in Oktibbeha County.

Jerry would go up on the swaying scaffolding with his dad and catch the bricks that were thrown up to him. "One of my brothers would stack about four bricks on top of each other and toss them up. They might go this way and that way, and I would catch all four." And until this day Joe maintains, "He handled bricks better than any worker I ever had. I was sorry to see him go." Even then, Jerry had the large, soft hands of a great wide receiver.

Jerry, though, was more interested in hitting the books than in hauling in footballs. "I was very shy, a loner. I hung out mostly at the house. I did my homework for school, but I had no goals in mind. I didn't know what I wanted to do. I just sort of existed. I figured I'd end up being an electrician or an auto mechanic, because I liked working with my hands. I could fix anything.

"I never played sports and I wasn't interested in them," he says, "I had a brother who played at Jackson State, so I followed football because of him. But I wasn't really excited about going out there and getting myself knocked around."

One day, at the beginning of his sophomore year at B. L. Moore High School, Jerry decided to cut class and was spotted by the vice principal. "He slipped up behind me and scared me," says Jerry. "I just took off running, and all he could see was a flash of red jacket."

The vice principal must have been a pretty fair talent scout, though, because after dishing out the usual punishment, he suggested that Jerry could put his speed to better use on the football field, and directed "Flash" to report to the football coach. And ever since then, defensive backs at all levels, from high school to the NFL, have been paying the price for Jerry's day of truancy.

Jerry's mom, Eddie, wasn't too thrilled with the idea of another of her sons playing such a rough sport. "But the more I fought it, the more determined he was, so I gave it up." Papa Joe, though, loved watching his boys play ball, and he still remembers the day that he realized that Jerry had a special talent.

"It was just fun to watch them, Tom, Jimmy, and Jerry. They were always after that football. One day I saw Jerry dive into a thorn bush after a ball. He got stuck bad, but he caught it. When I saw that, I felt something."

Jerry also tried to play baseball in high school, but quickly gave up on that sport. "I tried to play baseball in high school. But I couldn't stand at the plate and face a 90-mile-per-hour fastball. I'm thinking, 'How can I play football, and be afraid of a hardball?' I don't know, I don't know. But I couldn't hit the ball, so I guess that's why I chose another sport."

2 World

Jerry went on to become a high school gridiron star, snaring 35 touchdown passes in his senior year. But no college coaches came to beat down the Rices' door. Jerry was especially disappointed by the lack of interest shown by Mississippi State, which was located just a few miles down the road from the Rice home. "I grew up wanting to go to Mississippi State more than anything in the world. But they didn't even care enough to write." Jerry's short-term pain turned out to be State's long-term embarrassment, though, for allowing such a great talent to go unnoticed in their own backyard.

One school that did show a little interest was Mississippi Valley State, a small college about 100 miles away from Crawford in a town called Itta Bena. But the interest was so slight that Archie Cooley, the head coach at the time, didn't go to see Jerry play until the football season had finished and Jerry was already pounding the boards for Moor's basketball team.

But once Cooley saw Jerry's athleticism, he couldn't wait to see him in an MVS uniform. "I became impressed with him immediately. He could jump through the roof, and he had those huge hands. He got about 30 points that night, and right away I decided we had to have him."

Jerry's talents were perfectly suited to the offensive schemes of "Gunslinger" Cooley, whose motto was "The fastest way between two points is to fly."

And Jerry flew, catching 30 passes in his freshman year, and more than doubling that total in his sophomore season. "I just felt natural right away," said Jerry, who was nicknamed by his teammates "World," as in "All-World." "Then things just started getting easier." But the only reason that things got easier was because of how hard Jerry worked.

Jerry kept improving, because he wasn't content to rely on his natural speed and exceptional jumping ability. He participated in a sprinting program to improve his quickness and a weight-training program to increase his strength. Jerry also worked at developing his concentration and learning to run precise pass patterns. And you could usually find him running his route an hour before practice even officially began. This extra effort by Jerry wasn't at all surprising, for as his mother said, "He has worked hard at everything he's done all his life."

Jerry quickly became the marked man in the Delta Devil's offense, usually having to defeat double- or even triple-teaming, but he made it sound as though it was as easy to deal with as a quiet stroll through the park. "You've got to get rid of the first man, run the pattern on the second man, and take the ball away from the third man." Just like that.

And after Jerry had the ball, he was bad news for any defensive back who was between him and the goal line. "He came across the field with so much intensity that guys seemed like they were getting out of *his* way," remarked Gloster Richardson, the Delta Devils' receiving coach, and an ex-pro star with the Kansas City Chiefs. Jerry relished those open-field opportunities. "I'm always looking to turn it upfield and run over some people."

Jerry ran over lots of people while catching over one-hundred passes in *each* of his last two seasons, including an astounding 28 touchdown receptions in his senior year. By the time Jerry hung up his Delta Devils' cleats, he had set 18 NCAA Division 1-AA records, including career yardage and touchdown totals, and the pro scouts were paying a lot more attention then the college coaches had four year earlier.

Dick Steinberg, a longtime NFL talent evaluator and currently the general manager of the New York Jets, seemed to feel that there wasn't any limit to Jerry's potential. "You'd see him catch 10 in the first half, and you wondered if he could catch 30 in a game," said Steinberg with a straight face.

One of the teams that had particular interest in Jerry was the San Francisco 49ers. They were looking for a long-range wide receiver who could stretch defensive secondaries and take the pressure off the short-range passing schemes that Bill Walsh favored.

The 49ers sent Paul Hackett, an offensive assistant at the time, to watch Jerry work out with hundreds of other college seniors who had dreams of playing in the NFL. "Jerry was sensational. I couldn't believe what I was watching. I couldn't wait to get back to Bill and tell him what I'd seen."

The only problem was that the 49ers, coming off their win in Super Bowl XIX, would have the 28th pick in the 1985 NFL draft, too late to grab Jerry. So, on the day of the draft, Walsh traded the team's top three draft picks to the New England Patriots to move up in the draft and get their man.

Jerry, who had been watching the draft proceedings on TV with one of his brothers, was a little disappointed that he was only the third wide receiver chosen—after Al Toon, who was taken by the New York Jets and Eddie Brown, who was snared by the Cincinnati Bengals. But he was also thrilled about being selected by the NFL's top team. "My first thought was, 'Super Bowl champs. I'm going to get one of those rings myself.'"

3 Rookie

Jerry had the normal case of rookie shakes in his first season, as he tried to earn a starting spot on a veteran team. Jerry, though, also had to deal with being a long way from home for the first time, and adjusting to big-city ways after spending his entire life in small-town rural settings. "When I got here, things didn't really fall in place for me. I remember stepping off the plane. At that particular moment, I wanted to turn around and go back on the plane because of shyness. I had a hard time. I kept my head in the right frame of mind, though. If not for that, I'd probably be home in Mississippi."

Jerry handled the pressure with remarkable maturity and demonstrated, almost immediately, that his talents as a receiver were something special.

Paul Hackett remembers a catch that was so spectacular that, even though it was an exhibition game and Jerry came down out of bounds, he says, "I'll never forget it. He went up between three defenders, got bumped, and still came down with the ball. It seemed like he could just hang there in the air forever on that pass, waiting for the ball. It's one of the greatest catches I've ever seen."

"That first training camp, I remember distinctly how he intimidated many of our defensive backs to a point where they started off the season without any confidence," said head coach George Seifert, who at the time was the 49ers defensive coordinator.

Jerry also caught Joe Montana's attention in the first regular-season game when he went across the middle and made a great leaping catch. "Jerry showed everyone that he wasn't afraid to go across the middle—the most dangerous spot for a receiver—to catch a pass," said Montana, who was the 49ers' starting quarterback at the time.

The 49ers, though, brought Jerry along slowly, easing him into the lineup gradually so as to lessen the pressure on him. But despite the coaching staff's best-laid plans, Jerry still hit a mid-season patch in which he dropped a lot of catchable balls, causing his confidence to sag

"I started dropping passes in my sleep. It was tough to deal with. I couldn't concentrate on the football. I was thinking about the offense, my pattern, and what the defense was trying to do to me.

"It was a case of trying too bite off to much too soon. I came into the league wanting to prove to everybody that I could play on the professional level. Then they handed me this big playbook that was very complex. I had to learn to pick up so much about so many different situations. The thing I forgot to do was to catch the football. After I mastered the book, everything fell into place."

Jerry dealt with the situation head-on, working harder in practice and learning the offense more completely, so that he didn't have to continually think about what he was supposed to do and could just concentrate on beating his defender and catching the ball.

Jerry's efforts paid off so well that by the fourteenth game of the season, he grabbed 10 passes—including a 66-yard touchdown catch for a whopping 241 yards, a new 49er record. Steve Shafer, the Rams' defensive-backfield coach who had just seen his secondary get eaten alive, was dazzled by Jerry's exploits. "The thing he does is finish a play as well as anyone in football. He goes for the ball better than anybody, and he knows what to do with it when he catches it."

Jerry closed out the season with another big game against Dallas, and walked away with the United Press International Rookie of the Year Award. He was also selected the National Football League's Players' Association Offensive Rookie of the

Year. But his dream of winning a Super Bowl ring was short-circuited by the Giants in the opening round of the playoffs.

Jerry had shown the league that a new star was emerging, but without a crystal ball, no one would have guessed that he was about to ignite with all the brightness of a supernova.

4 Sophomore Sensation

For some unknown reason, a lot of professional athletes who have fine rookie seasons seem to slump in their second season. Aware of this phenomenon, Jerry spent the offseason working out and building himself up so that he wouldn't fall victim to the "Sophomore Jinx" for lack of effort.

Jerry did take some time off, though, to arrange to have a new home built for his parents. "They didn't have much when I was growing up, but all they had went to the kids. When I got to the NFL, I was determined to give something back to them," said Jerry.

Despite Jerry's offseason dedication and an excellent training-camp effort, it looked like the jinx was going to get Jerry anyway when Joe Montana went down with a back injury that would sideline him for half of the 49ers' 1986 schedule.

It takes a lot of experience for a receiver and quarterback to learn each other's moves and develop the timing and knowledge that allows them to work smoothly together. So the loss of a starting quarterback is usually a setback to any receiver, especially a young and relatively inexperienced wide receiver still trying to master the intricacies of a Bill Walsh offense.

But Jerry adapted to backup quarterbacks Jeff Kemp and Mike Moroski without appearing to miss a beat. In the 49ers' first game after the injury. Jerry hauled in six passes for 155 yards, including a 66-yard touchdown against the Rams. Jerry followed up that performance with a two-touchdown effort against the Dolphins, and two spectacular back-to-back beauties against the Colts and the Vikings in which he collected 13 passes good for 316 yards and five more touchdowns.

The speed with which Jerry turned into such a dangerous receiver startled even the 49ers. "There is no better player at his position right now than Jerry Rice," declared Walsh. "There are some as good, but none better. We always said that his best would come three or four years down the road, but he's surprised us all."

Joe Montana also caught everyone by surprise when he returned to the lineup in time for the 49ers' tenth game of the season. Jerry did his part to welcome Joe back by hauling in three touchdown passes and racking up 157 yards in receptions against the Phoenix Cardinals. It did more for Joe's spirits than a Hallmark card.

The following week the 49ers played in the nation's capitol, and Jerry had his biggest game of the season against Washington and their All-Pro cornerback, Darrell Green. Jerry made the speedy Green look like a confused rookie as he burned him 12 times for 204 yards, one of only two 200-plus-yards performances turned in by an NFL receiver in 1986. After the game a shame-faced Green admitted, "I'm embarrassed."

Jerry went on to embarrass a lot of other cornerbacks throughout the league, finishing the season with 86 receptions good for a league-leading 15 touchdown grabs and 1,570 receiving yards, the third highest total ever in the long history of the NFL.

Jerry's accomplishments earned him All-Pro honors and a selection as *Sports Illustrated's* NFL Player of the Year, a rare honor for a second-year performer.

"Jerry's become so good so fast, it scares you sometimes," said Dennis Green, the 49ers' receivers coach at the time. "He just explodes towards the ball. If a pass is near him, it's his. He just turns on the afterburners.

"And he has a basketball player's leaping ability. If he goes up in a crowd with two or three defenders, Jerry's going to get the ball. And if both of them grab it at once, Jerry will probably pull it away. He's a tough kid."

Tough enough, too to have beaten the sophomore jinx in a big, big way.

But it was a different story in the 49ers' playoff game against the Giants. The New Yorkers, who would go on to win the Super Bowl that year, just rolled over the 49ers and flattened them out, 49–3.

The game was a horror show for the 49ers from start to finish. For Jerry, though, there was one play that stood out like a bad dream. In the first quarter, the 49ers had the chance to strike first and take the early lead. They were in Giant territory and driving towards a touchdown as Jerry caught a slant-in pass and took off for the end zone. "I was actually pulling away from the defense and thinking about the touchdown giving us the lead."

But as Jerry crossed the 20-yard line, the ball simply fell out of his hand and rolled into the end zone, where a Giant player fell on it. "It just came out," said Jerry, speaking about the only ball he fumbled all year.

Most of the people who watched the game thought it was a bizarre but insignificant play, thinking that even if Jerry hadn't fumbled, the Giants were so dominating that the final score still wouldn't have been much closer than 49–10 anyway.

But some people, including Jerry, wonder whether that early score could have changed the momentum and the outcome of the game. "You tell yourself that you lost so badly that it doesn't matter, but you never know. That one play might have given us all we needed to win the game. That one play might have put us in the Super Bowl. It will always linger in the back of my mind." When he made his travel plans for the Pro-Bowl game, which is played in Hawaii the week after Super Sunday, he made sure that he'd be airborne while the Super Bowl was being televised. "I didn't want to know anything about that game."

Although Jerry's' sophomore year may have ended on a down note, one dropped ball couldn't obscure his season-long display of brilliance or slow his relentless pursuit of greatness.

5 Touchdown Machine

Instead of sitting around and brooding about the dropped ball, Jerry went to work getting ready for the 1987 season. He reported to training camp in great shape, ready to put in the time and effort that would allow him to take his game to the next level.

"Jerry's like everyone else," said Dennis Green, "But he works *hard*. He stays after practice day after day. The guy's always improving, and he's almost perfect now."

Ronnie Lott, who was Jerry's teammate at the time, a perennial All-Pro perfomer and a player who has always set the highest standards, also spoke admiringly of the way that Jerry went all out, even in practice. "Jerry's always at top speed. Young defensive backs want to avoid him in drills."

And then, comparing Jerry to two Hall of Fame receivers, Lott—one of the greatest defensive backs ever to play the game—added, "Covering Jerry in practice is the closest I'll ever come to covering a Paul Warfield or Charlie Taylor."

And the NFL Hall of Fame is where Jerry quickly set his sights. Jerry had a chance to visit the Hall when the 49ers opened their exhibition schedule with a game in Canton, Ohio, and he came away inspired. "It sent chills through me. That's where I want to go. I want to be in there with guys who didn't play for the money as much as for the challenge."

By the time the 1987 season was in the record books, Jerry would have clearly demonstrated that in only his third year in the NFL, he was already the equal of any of the immortals elected to the Hall of Fame.

Playing in only 12 games because of a players' strike, Jerry lived up to his nickname of "World" by setting a record for touchdown receptions, with 22. Jerry *shattered* the old standard of 18 touchdown receptions that former Miami Dolphin receiver Mark Clayton had established over a 16-game schedule in 1984, the year that Dan Marino was filling the air with footballs and throwing an NFL-record 48 touchdown passes.

Jerry's total of 23 touchdowns (he also ran one in on a reverse play against the Atlanta Falcons) left him one shy of the league record of 24, set by former Washington running back John Riggins, but the 138 points that he tallied did give him the NFL scoring title, the first time a wide receiver had led the league since Hall of Famer Elroy "Crazy Legs" Hirsch had done it in 1951.

Jerry's accomplishment was so awesome that people were searching for new adjectives to describe his all-world performance. Tim McKyer, his teammate at the time, captured the image as well as anyone. "You feed all the data of the ideal receiver into a computer and it spits out Jerry Rice."

Jerry also set another record by catching at least one touchdown in 13 consecutive games, including the last game of the 1986 season and all 12 games that he played in 1987. "For a receiver to have that kind of consistency is remarkable," said Jerry's boyhood idol, Lynn Swann, a former All-Pro on the Steelers' Super Bowl teams of the seventies. To Bill Walsh, in fact, the consecutive game streak was an even more outstanding achievement than the 23 touchdowns that Jerry had scored over 12 games.

"He's just got a great attitude. When he catches the ball, he's thinking TD," said Sherman Lewis a former 49ers receiving coach. "Every time he touches it, he's thinking about getting in the end zone. And because he thinks that way, it lots of times happens."

Jerry's fabulous season began in Pittsburgh, where the 49ers opened with a loss to the Steelers. After the game, Steeler cornerback Dwayne Woodruff seemed relieved that Jerry had caught only one touchdown pass against him. "Covering Rice is like a horror show. He's so smooth when he's running. He gets right on you, and before you know it, he's by you. And once he is, I don't think anybody's going to catch him."

Following four weeks of forced vacation because of the players' strike, Jerry kept his streak alive with one touchdown grab in each of the 49ers' next three games. And then Jerry closed with a fabulous finishing kick by scoring *16 touchdowns* in his last *seven games*. During that sensational stretch, in which the 49ers went undefeated, Jerry scored three touchdowns in three of the games and two more in three other games. Only one team, the Green Bay Packers, held him to a single touchdown in that span.

After Jerry burned the Tampa Bay Buccaneers for three touchdowns, their head coach, former NFL wide receiver Ray Perkins, didn't need to see any more. "He's the best receiver in football."

The following week's foe, the Cleveland Browns, hadn't become believers—yet. Before the game, Hanford Dixon, one of their two All-Pro cornerbacks, laid down the challenge. "We're going to stay in his face all day." That tough talk just made Jerry's teammate, Randy Cross, smile. "He's more confident when people say what they're going to try to do to him. It seems to goad him into playing better."

Then Jerry went out and proved Cross correct by burning the Browns for seven catches, including three more touchdown receptions, as the 49ers creamed Cleveland, 38–24. The only effective defense against Jerry was the game officials, who forced him to get rid of his good-luck towel, which had "Flash 80" written on it. "They took away my energy," said Jerry after the game. But then he found a way to restore his elixir by taping the message on the bottom of his cleats. And at least that way, Dixon and the rest of the league's cornerbacks had something to read while Jerry raced into the end zone.

Jerry's extraordinary efforts helped the 49ers achieve an NFL-best 13–2 record (including three wins by a team of strikebreakers that counted in the official standings). But for the third consecutive year, the 49ers were routed in their opening-round playoff game. This time the villain was the Vikings, and once again the 49ers' celebrated trio of scoring-stars—Montana, running back Roger Craig, and the Touchdown Machine, Jerry Rice—failed to produce a single score.

Montana took most of the heat from the fans and the media, especially after Walsh replaced him in mid-game with Steve Young. But Jerry, who played the game hampered by a pulled muscle and a bad knee, leaped to Montana's defense. "Everyone said Joe had a bad game. Well, *everybody* did. I had three or four balls that I didn't come down with that I should have had. It's disappointing to me that I didn't play better."

And even though Jerry was named the NFL's Most Valuable Player and the *Sporting News* NFL Player of the Year, as well as winning the Len Eshmont award which the 49er players give to the teammate that they select as being the most inspirational and courageous player on the team, the early elimination from the playoffs cut deeply. "The only thing I have to hang on to is the awards," said Jerry, "Because the season didn't end like I wanted it to."

It was beginning to look as though the only way Jerry was going to get to a Super Bowl was to buy a ticket.

6 Over the Hump

Jerry had roared like a lion during his first three seasons in the NFL, but had been as quiet as a mouse in the playoffs. He was disturbed at his, and at the team's poor performance in those three-straight postseason losses. When it had counted most, Jerry and the 49ers' other two offensive superstars, Montana and Craig, had produced the least. The trio had rewritten the record book during the previous three seasons, but had failed to produce a single touchdown in postseason play. In those three opening-round losses, Jerry had been limited to a total of only ten catches for 121 yards.

And after the 49ers foundered their way through the first 11 games of the 1988 season, it didn't look as though they would even make it to the playoffs. With a 6–5 record and only five games to go, their hopes were down to a faint flicker. The usually explosive offense of the 49ers sputtered as Joe Montana struggled through his most miserable and least productive season, while Jerry suffered an injury to his right ankle in the team's seventh game that hampered him for the remainder of the schedule.

Jerry, though, came up big in the 49ers' four-game stretch drive that turned their season around. Playing through the team's turmoil and the pain of his injured ankle, Jerry came up with four touchdown grabs, including a team-record 96-yarder, as the 49ers fought their way into the playoffs. Jerry's final statistics weren't as glittering as they had been in the two previous record-setting seasons, but they were good enough to earn him All-Pro honors for the third consecutive year.

The 49ers' first playoff obstacle was the Minnesota Vikings, the team that had eliminated them a year earlier and which had the NFL's top-rated defense. The 49ers, however, also had to overcome the cloud of doubt caused by their recent playoff failures.

Jerry quickly made sure that the sun shined brightly over San Francisco's Candlestick Park, though, by personally dismantling the league's dominant defense. Completely dispelling the idea that he wasn't a big-game performer, Jerry went out and tied a postseason record by scoring three times—all in the first half—to lead the 49ers past the Vikes 34–9.

The 49ers had put their playoff blues behind them, but waiting in Chicago to ambush their NFC championship hopes were the big bad Bears—and NFL history. Going back to 1950, there had been 19 games in which a warm-weather team or a team that played in a domed stadium had traveled to a cold-weather city to play for a championship. And 18 times in those 19 games, the team that played in the cold-weather city had walked off its field as a winner.

But Jerry wasn't interested in the past, or in the fact that the Bears had beaten the Niners 10–9 earlier in the season. "The first time we played the Bears this year, I had a bad ankle. I couldn't really move. But I'm healthy now and I'm going to have a big game tomorrow. You're going to see a different Jerry Rice tomorrow," he announced. Jerry also didn't allow a frigid weather forecast for the Windy City to bother him. "I don't care. I'll catch the ball in any kind of weather."

But Jerry wasn't expecting the extreme Arctic conditions that sent the temperature plunging below zero while swirling winds whipped the football around as though it was a wiffle ball. The elements seemed to dictate a low-scoring, defensive struggle without much passing. But midway through the first quarter, Jerry started delivering on his pregame promise.

On a third-down-and-ten from the 49ers own 39-yard line, Montana sent Jerry out on a 20-yard sideline pattern. Just before the pass reached Jerry, the ball seemed to soar on a sudden updraft like a Frisbee caught in the wind. But "World," looking like he had been launched, went right up after the ball and snatched it out of the air, and away from Chicago cornerback Mike Richardson. The catch was already a great play, but Jerry wasn't finished. As soon as his feet touched the ground, he put a fantastic fake on Todd Krumm, who had come over to make the tackle, and—*whoosh*—Jerry was gone, 61 yards, for the game's opening score.

In the second quarter, Jerry kept a drive alive by taking a short pass and turning it into a 20-yard gain. Five plays later, from the Bears' 27-yard line, Jerry, running a short slant-in pattern, snatched a knee-high bullet pass with his fingertips and sprinted the final 15 yards into the end zone. The touchdown gave the 49ers a 14–0 lead and they went on to put the Bears in the deep freeze in a big way, 28–3.

Jerry had beaten the playoff jinx for the second time, withstood the worst weather conditions he had ever played in, and completely devastated Chicago's defense. Now the only thing standing between Jerry and his Super Bowl ring was the Cincinnati Bengals.

7 Going for the Ring

The weather in Miami, the site of Super Bowl XXIII, was a big improvement over what the 49ers had faced in Chicago. But the barrage of bad-mouthing that the Bengals'defensive backs heaped on Jerry was as welcoming as an Alaskan blizzard.

The Bengals' secondary, which billed itself as "the Swat Team," kept bragging to the media that they would throw a blanket over Jerry. "We'll play a lot of bump-and-run," said Cincinnati cornerback Lewis Billups. "He won't be able to handle that." And strong safety David Fulcher added, "All of us are faster than he is."

"This isn't a track meet. It's a football game," answered Jerry, who had been hearing about his lack of speed for a long time.

His supposed lack of speed was one of the reasons that he hadn't been highly recruited by colleges, and why wide receivers Al Toon and Eddie Brown had been picked ahead of him in the 1985 draft.

Jerry has never liked to run in shorts against a clock, so he doesn't do the 4.2-second times that coaches like to see for a wide receiver. But in full football gear, running a pass pattern with the ball out in front of him, Jerry becomes a *burner*. As Ronnie Lott noted, "Jerry's got game speed. It's hard to explain, but *nobody* outruns Jerry in a game."

Most people expected Super Bowl XXIII to be a high-scoring game that would be dominated by two explosive offenses. But the expected fireworks frizzled early, and the teams went to their locker rooms tied at 3–3.

Jerry, with a series of acrobatic catches that were all highlight-film material including a one-handed sideline grab of a tipped ball, had put on a truly awesome display of pass catching in the first half. But a disputed dropped pass by Mike Wilson at the Bengals' two-yard line, a botched field goal attempt, and a fumble by Roger Craig had undercut Jerry's efforts to put more points on the scoreboard.

Those miscues looked as though they might prove fatal, when the Bengals broke a 6–6 tie with a dramatic 93-yard kickoff return by Stanford Jennings with less than a minute left in the third quarter. But before Cincinnati could take control of the game, Jerry, with major contributions from Joe Montana and Roger Craig, broke the Bengals' momentum.

On the first play from scrimmage after Jennings' touchdown jaunt, Jerry took a short sideline pass from Montana, spun away from a tackle, and turned it into a 31-yard gain. On the next play, the first of the fourth quarter, Montana connected with Craig on a 40-yard gain to take the ball to the Bengals' 14-yard line. One play later, Jerry gathered in a sideline pass in the left flat at the Bengals' five-yard line. As soon as Jerry caught the ball, Billups banged him in the back and sent him sprawling across the end line. But just before Jerry fell out of bounds, he somehow lunged forward while reaching back with his right hand and arched the football around the pylon in the corner of the end zone, to pull the 49ers into a 13–13 tie. As the 49ers' receivers coach Dennis Green said admiringly, "Everything was out of bounds except the ball."

Jerry made another unbelievable catch on the 49ers' next possession as he exploded into the air over "He won't be able to handle that" Billups and brought down a 44-yard rainmaker. The 49ers wasted that opportunity, though, when Mike Cofer missed a 49-yard field-goal attempt. But the extraordinary play that Jerry had made in scoring the tying touchdown on the previous series had given the 49ers the platform from which to spring back after Cincinnati retook the lead, 16–13, with only 3:20 left to play. The 49ers used that opportunity to execute a 92-yard scoring drive to win the most exciting Super Bowl ever played.

In that drive, Jerry caught three passes that contributed 51 yards, including a key 27-yarder on a second-down-and-20 play that moved the ball to the Bengals' 18-yard stripe with less than a minute left to play in the game. "I love to be in a situation like that, where everything is on the line. I want to be the guy to come up with the catch," said Jerry.

Two plays later, with the Bengals' defense keying on Jerry with double team coverage, John Taylor was able to get free in the end zone, where he cradled the Montana pass that won Super Bowl XXIII for the 49ers.

Taylor readily acknowledges the fact that his teammate had opened up the passing lane for him. "Everyone in the place was probably looking at Jerry, not at me." Which was not surprising, since Jerry had tied one Super Bowl record with his 11 catches—including three that were in the category of unbelievable—and set a new mark with 215 receiving yards. Including the Vikings and Bears games, Jerry had caught 21 passes for 409 yards and a record-tying six postseason touchdowns. No one would ever say that Jerry couldn't play in the big games again.

After Jerry left the field, he went to his locker and wept forcefully for a few minutes, mentally retracing the long, hard road that he had traveled to achieve this moment. He remembered the hard times early in his rookie year, and he remembered catching bricks out of the air, and his hard-working parents, who had loved and supported him throughout out his life.

"Just the other day, for some reason, I was thinking about working with my father. It was strange because I started to smile. He's been on my mind a lot lately, thinking about those long, hard days we worked together. He'd get me up around 6 o'clock in the morning and we'd get in at 5 o'clock at night. When I was doing that, I thought it was the worst thing possible. But looking back, I know it made me a better person. For one thing, I learned I had to work hard to achieve anything in life."

Then Jerry wiped his eyes and joined his celebrating teammates just in time to learn that he had been selected as the Most Valuable Player in the Super Bowl. Jerry modestly suggested that Montana might have been a better choice, but no one was more deserving than Jerry. As Ronnie Lott put it, "I've said all along that Jerry Rice is the best wide receiver ever to play the game. Yes, ever." And he saved one of his best performances for the most important game that he had ever played.

Jerry joined Lynn Swann (for the Steelers in Super Bowl X) and Fred Biletnikoff (for the Raiders in Super Bowl XI) as the only wide receivers to ever win the MVP award. "Lynn Swann was my idol," said Jerry. "It amazed me how he would fly through the air and make catches."

But these days it's Swann who is doing the admiring. "There isn't a wide receiver who has played a better Super Bowl to date, and that includes me," said Swann, after watching Jerry soar to new heights.

Over in the Bengals' locker room , the Swat Team was still talking, but this time with respect instead of derision. "I should have played better, I guess," said Billups. "But Rice made a couple of super catches when I was right on him. I was right on him and he *still* made the catches."

David Fulcher swiftly summed up his reaction to Jerry's record-smashing performance. "Jerry Rice is in another world at times."

When Jerry was asked to comment on all the trash talk the Bengals' defensive backs had thrown his way, he just smiled and said, "I don't talk a game; I just go out and play."

And according to Dwight Clark, for one, Jerry plays wide receiver better than anyone who ever played the position. "The first time I saw him, he was the best I ever saw, and I learned how to turn on the television at an early age. Jerry's like a Michael Jordan. He's a step above the field."

There was a negative incident in the postgame celebration when Jerry felt that he wasn't getting all the respect that he deserved. Although he took some heat for his words and at other times during his career, Jerry doesn't flinch when he feels he has something to say. "That's the way I was brought up, and I'm not going to change now. I would hate to think that I saw something wrong and didn't speak up."

8 Getting Better All the Time

After only four seasons in the league, Jerry was already being favorably compared with the greatest receivers of all time. He had put his special stamp on each of his seasons: winning Rookie of the Year honors in his first season; achieving the third-highest receiving yardage total in NFL history in his second year; establishing the record for touchdown receptions in a season and being named the NFL's MVP during his third year; and being named the Most Valuable Player in Super Bowl XXIII in his fourth season.

Jerry, though, didn't have any interest in resting on his accomplishments and admiring his trophy case. "I don't want to stop and think about my individual achievements, or it might distract me," said Jerry, whose major focus is on helping the 49ers win as many championships as possible, and one day, a long time down the road, being elected to the NFL Hall of Fame. "I still need to work on improving my abilities, like in reading defenses. I'm still not sharp doing that."

Superstars like Jerry or Michael Jordan aren't interested in what they've already done; they stoke their competitive fires by stepping forward to meet the next set of challenges. And they're constantly working to develop their natural talents to their fullest potential.

So instead of allowing his head to swell with praise during the offseason, Jerry cut back on the junk food that he loves and lost 15 pounds, because he decided that he could improve his quickness if he was lighter. And to make sure that he didn't lose strength as a result of the lost weight, Jerry put in a lot of time in the weight room, bulking up his body. "You see a lot of guys that catch the ball just fall down to the ground. But that's something we [Jerry and his teammate and fellow wide receiver, John Taylor] try to stay away from. If we catch the football, we're going to do something with it."

And Jerry started doing things on the opening day of the 1989 season when he caught a pass and galloped 58 yards to give the 49ers a come-from-behind win over the Colts, 30–24.

That win set the tone for the Niners' best-in-the-NFL 14–2 season. Jerry also went on to have another monster year, compiling league highs in receiving yardage (1,483) and touchdown receptions (17), including scores that put the winning points on the board in five of the Niners' 14 wins.

Jerry also set the tone for the team's drive to Super Bowl XXIV in its opening playoff contest against Minnesota. After the Vikes jumped out to a 3–0 first quarter lead, Jerry turned the game around with a 72-yard score that sucked the air out of the Vikings' top-rated defense.

The play started off as a simple five-yard hook pass, and finished in the end zone, as Jerry turned on the retro rockets after blasting his way out of the grasp of two would-be tacklers. The Vikes, thinking that they were watching an instant replay of what Jerry had done to them in the 1988 play-offs, reacted as if they were in a trance.

"The defense went into shock after that play," admitted Floyd Peters, who was the Vikings' defensive coordinator. "It was a total collapse."

Jerry made sure that the Minnesota defense remained stunned by catching a 13-yard touchdown pass that increased the 49ers' half-time lead to 27–3 and putting the game out of the Viking's reach.

Jerry didn't play the starring role in the Niners' NFC championship win over the Rams, but he was the game's leading receiver and he kept the Rams' secondary so preoccupied with his whereabouts that it opened up field for the other 49er players. And Jerry, who is probably the league's best blocking wide receiver, also helped by throwing a couple of bone-crushing blocks that twice sprang Roger Craig for big-yardage gains.

The scene of Super Bowl XXIV switched from Miami to New Orleans, but the Denver Broncos' secondary sang the same old song that the Bengals' defensive backs had sung prior to Super Bowl XXIII. This time around, free safety Steve Atwater, the NFL's defensive Rookie of the Year, and Dennis Smith, Denver's Pro-Bowl-caliber strong safety, two of the league's hardest hitters, provided the lyrics.

"We're going to beat up Rice and Taylor a bit," Smith told reporters. "They really haven't been hit a lot in the play offs. But when they catch a ball against us, they're going to remember it.

"Rice is a great athlete, no doubt about it. He has that fifth gear where most people only have four. But we're just going to go out there and strip some of those gears."

Jerry, hearing what was said, shot right back. "I'm ticked off. It's the same as Cincinnati last year. They talked and talked, and this game is not about talking."

With less than five minutes gone in the contest, Jerry showed everyone just what the game *was* about. With the ball at the Denver 20, Jerry ran a slant-in pattern and caught a pass in full stride at the seven-yard line, where Atwater tried to take his head off with a flying tackle. But Jerry bounced out of the safety's grasp, juked past another defender, and ran in for the score. "I just tried to keep my balance and focus on getting into the end zone," said Jerry. "This team expects me to make a big play to get things started. I focused on that and nothing else.

"We made our minds up that we weren't going down on the first hit today. It felt awfully good."

Forty-niners' offensive lineman Jesse Sapolu offered a free postgame public service announcement to all future 49er Super Bowl opponents. "I think everyone should learn one thing. Don't say anything about Rice before you have to play against him in a Super Bowl."

Two possessions later, the 49ers went 54 yards in ten plays to up their lead to 13–3. Jerry didn't score the touchdown, but he did set it up with two big receptions, a 20-yarder, and then a 21-yarder to dig the Niners out of a third-down hole.

Roger Craig and fullback Tom Rathman did all the work on the 49ers' third scoring drive, with Rathman ramming the ball in from the one-yard line.

Jerry got back into the scoring column just before the half ended, on a 38-yard touchdown play that had the Broncos shaking their heads. Faking a slant-in, which drew the over-anxious Denver secondary up, Jerry instead ran a deep post-pattern behind an outclassed Dennis Smith and caught a perfect spiral to give the 49ers a 27–3 half-time lead.

Over on the sidelines, Wade Phillips, Denver's frustrated defensive coordinator, was thinking, "We worked on that play every day in practice. We knew it was coming and we still couldn't stop it."

Two minutes into the third quarter, Jerry struck again, catching a 28-yard touchdown toss that upped the 49ers' lead to 34–3 and shut the door on any hopes that Denver had of coming back. "I was all pumped up for Denver. Their big safeties had been boasting that they were going to shut me down and knock me silly. But my three touchdowns shut them up."

"We just couldn't handle them," confessed Wade Phillips after the 49ers had finished demolishing Denver, 55–10. But no one has learned how to handle Jerry, who seems like a cobra, able to mesmerize his prey before striking with deadly quickness.

Jerry, who at that time owned eight Super Bowl records, was as usual, modest about his individual achievements but excited about what his team had accomplished. "Records are just thin print in fat books. Maybe the records will mean more to me in the future. But the most important thing is winning games. And to win back-to-back Super Bowls for this football team—that's what's important."

Other people, though, including the 49ers' offensive coordinator at the time, Mike Holmgren, who is now the coach of the Packers, wanted to talk about Jerry's greatness. "Jerry is still young, and as hard as it is to believe, I think his best years are ahead of him. He can get better, and that's a little scary."

Actually, it was a lot scary if you happened to be an opposing defensive back or coach and heard Jerry talking about scaling new heights while he was still standing in the locker room after his second consecutive record-setting Super Bowl performance.

"There's always room for improvement," said Jerry, who along with former Giants linebacker Lawrence Taylor and ex-Bengals offensive tackle Anthony Muñoz, were the only three unanimous selections to the NFL's All-1980's First Team. "I'm looking down the road. If you want to keep getting better, you have to set high standards for yourself."

And the standards that Jerry had already set for himself were the all-time records that Steve Largent had set in his 14 seasons with the Seattle Seahawks. Largent left the game following the 1989 season as the NFL's career leader in receptions (816), receiving yardage (13,035) and touchdown receptions (100). "I'm shooting for one guy. and that's Steve Largent. I feel that if I keep working hard and just keep down to earth, I might have a chance of surpassing him one day."

Those were the targets that Jerry had set his sights on, and five years into his career he was on course to achieving his goals and ultimately to gaining recognition as the greatest receiver ever to play the game of football.

"I know that some people are starting to say that I'm already the best," said Jerry, "but I don't think you can say that. Largent was a great receiver. He leads the list in yards, receptions, and in touchdowns. He paid the price. He deserves to be recognized that way. But maybe, if I get those records, I'll be able to accept it when people tell me that.

"But for now, I don't want to hear about it , because I still have too much to learn."

9 End of An Era

Although he was already recognized as the best wide receiver in the game and verged on being considered the best ever to play the game, Jerry stepped up his already rigorous offseason workout regime, and came to the 49ers training camp in 1990 with the attitude that he had to earn his starting position.

"I can't tell myself I've got it made. I still have to prove myself every year," said Jerry, expressing the mindset of a true champion.

Jerry, who was also fueled by a desire to help the 49ers achieve an unprecedented third straight Super Bowl victory, started the 1990 season by catching a TD pass in three of the team's first four games. In the team's third game Jerry lit up the Falcons for 171 yards at Candlestick Park. So two weeks later, when the 49ers traveled to Atlanta for a rematch, Jerry Glanville, the Falcons coach at the time, tried to disrupt the Niners' passing game by blitzing a defensive back or two on almost every play. The major problem with that strategy was that it allowed Jerry to operate one-on-one for most of the day against Atlanta cornerback Charles Dimry. By the end of the game Jerry had fried the Falcons for 13 catches, 225 yards, and an NFL record-tying five TD receptions. And Dimry had been burnt so often that he was nicknamed "Toast."

"Just another day at work, that's about it," said Jerry, trying to play down his super-duper day. "The important thing is that we won the football game. I don't sit around and swell on what I achieve, I just try to work hard.

"I think the reason everything turned out so well is that I've worked hard to learn how to read defenses. I know if the free safety leaves the middle, Joe's going to go to me. It's amazing, really, how much easier it is to play the game if you prepare properly.

"Every ball that Joe threw, I knew he was going to me because I could read the free safety. Joe and I were on the same wavelength for the entire game."

After an off game against the Steelers, Jerry posted a score in each of the next three games, while averaging over 140 receiving yards per contest. The 49ers, meanwhile, were flying high with a 9–0 record, right on track for their expected Super Bowl Three-peat.

The only cloud on the horizon was that their offense was out of balance, tops in the league in passing but only third from the bottom when it came to running the ball. So coach Seifert decided to emphasize the ground game, but in the process Jerry's role was diminished, his numbers dropped, and he went four games without getting the ball into the end zone.

The Niners were still rolling along, their record at 12–1, and Jerry didn't want to rock the boat. But he did make it known that he was feeling like the odd man out. "He just wants the ball," noted Montana. "And he just gets upset when he doesn't get it. You can always tell a great player because they always want the ball and in any situation, and Jerry is a great, great football player."

Jerry quickly got his wishes answered and he went on a season-ending tear that took him to the top of the league in receiving yardage (with 1,502), and in receptions (with 100), making him only the fourth player in NFL history to crack the century mark, and also earned him *Sports Illustrated* NFL Player of the Year honors.

The 49ers had finished at the top as a team with a league-best record of 14–2, and were the odds-on choice to become the first franchise to win three consecutive Super Bowls. The Niners took the first step toward that goal by whacking Washington 28–10 in a divisional playoff game in which Jerry chipped in with his twelfth career postseason TD reception, which tied the record that had been held by former Steeler receiver John Stallworth.

Next up for the Niners was the New York Giants, a hard-nosed team who had surrendered a league-low 211 points. The Niners had managed to squeak by the visiting Giants 7–3 during the regular season, and despite the Giants' fierce pass rush and double-teaming of both Jerry and John Taylor, they were ahead again, 13–9, late in the fourth quarter of the NFC Conference Championship Game.

But then the 49ers' fortunes started to ebb as Montana, who had been knocked down throughout the day, was sacked so hard that he was forced to the sidelines for the rest of the game. Although no one realized it at the time, Montana's exit from the contest would mark the end of an era.

A minute after Montana was knocked out of the game the Giants kicked a field goal that sliced the 49ers' lead to 13–12. The 49ers, with Steve Young now in as quarterback, still had the lead and the ball, and looked as if they just were going to run out the clock. But with only 2:36 left in the game, Giants' tackle Erik Howard jarred the ball out of the grasp of the usually sure-handed Roger Craig, and then Giants' linebacker Lawrence Taylor swooped over and snatched the ball out of the air to give the Giants one last chance.

The visitors worked the ball into field goal position and then, with only four seconds showing on the Candlestick Park scoreboard, Giants' Kicker Matt Bahr booted the ball through the uprights to give the Giants a 15–13 win, and end the Niners' dream of Three-peating.

10 Transition Time

Jerry knew that 1991 wasn't going to rank as one of his all-time favorite years as soon as it was announced that Montana had undergone season-ending elbow surgery.

The absence of Montana put a monkey-wrench in the 49ers' well-oiled offensive machine. The entire scheme was built around a precision passing game and Montana was the most precise passer in NFL history. Montana's absence was especially difficult for Jerry, who had developed such an on-field rapport with the quarterback that at times it seemed as though they could read each other's minds.

With Steve Young at quarterback, the passing game suffered, Young wasn't as accurate a passer as Montana. Also, he was a left-handed passer and therefore the ball had a different spin than if it had been thrown by a right-hander. "There's a different rotation on the ball," explained Jerry. "Somehow the ball seems to angle in a different direction. It can be distracting, and in a game just a little lack of concentration can cost you some catches. So with Steve, I'm constantly reminding myself to watch the ball all the way into my hands."

Then there was the fact that Steve threw a "hard" ball that was more difficult to catch than the "soft" passes thrown by Montana. Perhaps the biggest difference, though, was that Montana was an experienced and patient quarterback who took the time to let plays develop. And he was so familiar with the offensive schemes that even if the primary receiver was covered, Montana knew exactly where the secondary receiver was going to be. And more often than not, even when the first two options had been defensed, Montana would calmly scan the field and deliver the ball to a receiver who had been only the third option on that play.

Steve, on the other hand, did not have Montana's experience, knowledge of the game, or patience. As soon as he saw that the primary receiver was covered, Steve would usually pull the ball down and scramble for as much yardage as he could gain. And while he did manage to amass 415 rushing yards, second highest on the team, that's not the way the 49ers' offense was designed to operate. All that scrambling was disruptive to a receiving corps that was accustomed to being a part of the best passing game in the NFL.

To make matters worse, the 49ers staggered out of the starting gate by losing four of their first six games. Although Jerry was making big plays, averaging nearly 100 yards a game while scoring seven touchdowns, he was only averaging five catches a game. Even more importantly, the 49ers, who had been the NFL's winningest team since Jerry's arrival in San Francisco, were near the bottom of the league's standings.

Just about the time that the team finally started to turn its season around, Jerry became hampered by a slightly torn knee ligament and went through a span of five games in which he totaled only 19 catches for just 161 yards—and not a single touchdown. That was his most unproductive stretch of games since he had become a full-time starter at the end of his rookie season.

Jerry righted himself over the final four games of the season, however, making 27 catches for 427 yards and six touchdowns, while helping the Niners to close the season with a six-game winning streak. But even with that sprint to the finish line— which had been directed in large part by Steve Bono, the third-string QB who had stepped in when Steve Young had been sidelined by a knee injury in the ninth game of the season—the 49ers' 10–6 record wasn't good enough to stop them from being excluded from the playoff picture for the first time since 1980.

Jerry's numbers were good enough to put him among the NFL's leading receivers, and he also hit a number of important milestones, including moving into third place on the all-time career touchdown list, but it was far from a vintage year for the great wide receiver. In fact, it was the most frustrating season in his seven-year career, because it was the first time that he had been shut out of postseason play.

"It leaves a bad taste in your mouth to miss the playoffs. We just didn't play like the 49ers. We didn't go out and jump on opposing teams. I'd like to get back to the point where whenever we took the field the opposing team was scarred."

The Niners remained a team in turmoil during the offseason. There was constant tension regarding the quarterback situation throughout the spring and early summer, with Montana expected to make a full recovery and reclaim his starting role— while Young, who had been the NFL's top-rated passer in 1991, insisted that he deserved the right to compete for the number-one spot. The 49ers' president, Carmen Policy came within a whisker of resolving the controversy by swapping Steve to the Raiders for wide receiver Tim Brown. But the 49ers decided to retain Steve, which turned out to be very fortunate, since injuries limited Montana's play to the second half of the season's final game.

The team also looked as though it was about to do the unthinkable and part company with Jerry because the two sides couldn't come to an agreement over a new contract. Policy, in fact, went so far as to say that Jerry's career in San Francisco was finished.

The two sides finally agreed to compromise on a contract in late August. The new deal paid Jerry $7.8 million over three years, making the prized wide receiver the highest paid nonquarterback in the NFL at that time. Because the dispute took so long to resolve, however, Jerry missed all of training camp, and despite his vigorous offseason workout schedule, he wasn't in top football shape. That lack of readiness caused Jerry to struggle through the first half of the 1992 season. There were other factors that contributed to his sluggish start, such as a concussion that sidelined him for most of one game; a broken leg suffered by John Taylor, which increased the double coverages faced by Jerry; the fact that offensive coordinator Mike Shanahan wanted to diversify the team's offense; and the continuing lack of synchronization between Jerry and Steve Young.

But the bottom line was that after eight games, Jerry had gone over the 100 yard mark only once and had scored only four touchdowns, while averaging under five receptions per game. That minimal production caused Jerry to begin wondering if he was past his prime.

"You ask yourself if you can still get the job done, if the speed and the toughness is still there, if you can do the things that you did back when you were 23," said Jerry, who had just turned 30. "You have that doubt back there."

Jerry quickly put those doubts aside, however, with a second-half surge that spiked his numbers up and allowed him to achieve one of his major goals by overtaking Steve Largent as the NFL's all-time leader in touchdown receptions.

Jerry first caught Hall of Famer Don Huston, who had totaled 99 TD catches in his fabulous career with Green Bay. Huston, who played for the Packers from 1935 to 1945, when the NFL season was only 11 games long, was such a dominant player that he set records that are still standing a half a century later including: most seasons leading the league in receptions (8), most seasons leading the league in touchdown receptions (9), and most seasons leading the league in reception yardage (7).

Jerry bagged his 99th TD catch with a 42-yarder against the Rams in the 11th game of the season which Mike Shanahan described as "Unbelievable. That ball was underthrown, and he not only comes back to get it, but he also finds a way to score. Unbelievable," repeated Shanahan, recalling how Jerry had snatched the ball away from one defender at the five-yard line and then carried another one into the end zone.

Jerry upped his touchdown total to 100 the following week against the Eagles, and earned the admiration of their All-Pro cornerback, Eric Allen. "He still has the tenacity that sets him apart from the other receivers. Some guys do it with grace or strictly speed. But Jerry has a lot of heart and that's what makes him the best."

The 49ers next game was played in a hard-driving rain and a bone-chilling wind which whipped across the Candlestick Park Field. But neither the weather nor the Miami Dolphin defense was going to keep Jerry from catching his 101st touchdown pass and becoming the NFL's all-time leader in TD receptions.

Jerry, who doesn't normally dwell on records, was all pumped up for this one. "When they called my number I said to myself, 'If Steve throws the football to me, I'm going to go up and make the catch. No way is the defensive back going to separate me from the ball.'" And true to his promise, Jerry beat Dolphin cornerback J. B. Brown on a 12-yard slant pattern to become the all-time touchdown reception leader.

"I've been chasing the record a long time and I'm just glad to get it done," said Jerry, who took less than eight full seasons and only 121 games to break a record that had taken Largent 14 seasons and 190 games to set. Nineteen-ninety-two turned out to be a very tough year for Largent, whose other major records where surpassed by James Lofton (in career yardage), and by Art Monk (for career receptions).

The entire 49ers team ran into the end zone to offer their congratulations to Jerry, but no one was happier for him than Steve Young. "What a thrill," said Steve. "They tried to play a single coverage against him. The guy never had a chance."

Jerry also reached a number of other milestones in the Miami game, as he moved into the number-nine position on the career receptions list with 593, took over the fifth spot in career touchdowns with 106 (which included three rushing TD's), and became only the ninth receiver to go over 10,000 yards in career receptions.

"He's in a class by himself," declared Dolphins' coach Don Shula, who has played and/or coached with and against all the great receivers, other than Don Huston.

Jerry kept adding his name to the record book in two playoff games, a win against Washington and an NFC Championship Game loss to Dallas. By the end of the game against the Cowboys, Jerry owned the NFL postseason career records for receptions (75) and touchdowns (13), and he had tied John Stallworth's record for the most games with a 100 or more receiving yards (5).

But despite his awesome long-term accomplishments and his very respectable totals for the 1992 season, there was a growing sense that Jerry's best years were behind him. His 84 receptions, while the fourth highest total in the league, were 16 catches below the high-water mark of 100 that he had reached two years earlier. His 10 TD receptions, which would be a banner harvest for most wide receivers, was Jerry's lowest total since 1988 and the second lowest of his career. And likewise, his 1,201 receiving yards, which did rank him third in the league, was the lowest number of yards he had ever posted—excepting his rookie year and the 12-game strike-shortened 1987 season.

Jerry, though, wasn't about the accept the notion that he had passed his peak and was about to enter the downside of his career. "I feel like I'm still getting better. I feel like I could play another 10 seasons or so," he declared.

11 Back on Top

Despite Jerry's brave words, he didn't do anything in the early part of the 1993 season to suggest that he was anything more than merely one of the NFL's better receivers, rather than the premiere player at his position.

The 49ers also got off to a shaky win-one, lose-one start, and Jerry became vexed at the team's mediocre performance and what he considered to be his reduced role in the 49ers' offensive schemes.

The situation came to a head after the Niners dropped a 26–17 decision in Dallas that put their record at 3–3. Jerry saw the 49ers' season slipping off the edge, and he also read the stories that said that the Cowboys' Michael Irvin—who had a big time game against the 49ers—as well as Atlanta's Andre Rison and Green Bay's Sterling Sharpe had all passed Jerry in the rankings of the NFL's top receivers.

The idea that Jerry had slipped a notch immediately lit the fuse of his competitive fires, and set him off on an explosive eight game surge in which he caught 49 passes for 937 yards and 11 touchdowns.

"Those negative stories made me elevate my game," said Jerry, who sparked the 49ers to seven wins in his eight-game rampage, which completely turned their season around. "You come into this league trying to establish yourself so that you can say, 'Hey, this is my territory.' And all of a sudden people were saying that Michael, Andre, and Sterling were all better than me. You will never hear me say I'm the greatest, but I didn't think my game had dropped off at all. Suddenly, though, they were poaching in my territory, so I just had to go out and work even harder."

Jerry worked so hard that he went over the 100-yard receiving mark five times in his eight-game streak, including a scorching 172-yard, four-touchdown effort that decimated the

Tampa Bay secondary.

"He's a freak," said an admiring Floyd Peters, the Bucs' defensive coordinator. "Most receivers are blessed with some combination of speed, a little height, extraordinary athleticism, and great hands. But they won't have all of them. He does. Guys like Rice, Jim Brown and the other true greats, they only come down the pike once in a great while. "I've tried defensing Rice throughout his career, and he's just driven me crazy."

Jerry ended his eight-game binge with a 132-yard game against Detroit, after which Lions' cornerback Harry Colon offered his opinion about what made Jerry the game's most dangerous receiver. "Because of his fantastic work ethic he's running at the same speed in the fourth quarter that he did in the first. He just has such great stamina."

Ray Crockett, Detroit's other cornerback, also gave his take on what makes Jerry so unique. "He never lets up on a play. Most receivers kind of slack off if they're not the intended receiver, so you only have to play them when they're the primary receiver. But you have to stay with Rice on every play, because he's going to run an aggressive route even if he isn't the primary receiver."

Jerry, unlike most wide receivers, is also an aggressive blocker who is generally conceded to be the best blocking wide receiver in the league. It's a role in which he takes a great deal of pride, and, in fact, one of the games that stands out most vividly in Jerry's memory was a game against the Rams in which he caught only two passes, but twice threw blocks that leveled Rams' defenders and allowed John Taylor to score a pair of long-range touchdowns.

"When I look back at my career and go over my most distinct memories, it will be a game like that one that I'll relish. It's not just about getting into the end zone, it's also about making plays like that for my teammates."

It was during Jerry's eight-game explosion that he and Steve Young finally fine-tuned their timing and began working together as smoothly as Jerry had with Montana, who had been traded to the Kansas City Chiefs prior to the start of the 1993 season.

"I think Steve and I are making big progress now," said Jerry. "And I think we're going to get even better down the road. We talk about situations while we're on and off the field. When you communicate like that, you get to know what the other person is thinking and how they'll react to specific game situations."

By the end of the season they were such a productive duo that Steve was the league's leading passer and Jerry had re-established himself as the game's top receiver by snaring 98 passes for an NFL-high 1,503 receiving yards, making him the only player in league history to exceed 1,000 yards in receiving in eight consecutive seasons. Jerry was also tops in the NFL in touchdowns with 16. His extraordinary efforts earned him the selection as the 1993 NFL Offensive Player of the Year by the Associated Press, as well as his second Len Eshmont Award.

And then Jerry gave opposing defenses some offseason nightmare material when he declared, "I'm convinced that I still haven't reached my full potential. I can still learn, I can still get better. "I'm just not ready for anyone to take over my territory. The time will come. But it won't be for awhile."

Jerry had one major objective for the 1994 season, to help the 49ers regain their status as Super Bowl champions. As a first step in that direction he agreed to restructure his salary so that the team could afford to sign the free-agent defensive players that they would need to make a serious run at the title.

Then Jerry helped set a positive example by reporting two days early to the 49ers' training camp. "If you want to stay at a certain level, you've got to pay the price," explained Jerry.

Jerry, who was entering his tenth season with 124 touch-downs, putting him in the third place on the NFL's career touchdown list behind Hall of Fame running backs Walter Payton, who had tallied 125 TD's in his 13 years with the Chicago Bears, and Jim Brown, who had totaled 126 touchdowns in his nine seasons with the Cleveland Browns.

Jerry made no bones about how thrilled he was to be in a position to pass Payton and Brown. "When I think of it, it's amazing that I've been in the end zone almost as many times as they have. I certainly would like to have the record. " But he didn't want to let an individual accomplishment interfere with the team's attention span.

"I think it's very important that we try to get it done early, so the record chase doesn't become a big distraction," said Jerry. "Get it done, get it out of the way and focus on the goal we really want to achieve, which is to win ball games and try to get back to the Super Bowl."

Jerry made sure that the 49ers would keep their eyes on the big prize by striking for the three touchdowns that he needed to put him over the top in the 49ers' season-opening Monday Night game against the LA Raiders.

Jerry bagged his first score of the game on a 69-yard pass from Steve Young, and his second one on a 23-yard reverse from running back Ricky Watters. Then, late in the fourth quarter, Jerry outjumped a pair of Raider defenders at the two-yard line, tore the ball out of the air, and fought his way into the end zone with his record-breaking 127th touchdown.

"I was really happy to get it," said Jerry, who tearfully raced over to the stands where his wife, Jackie, and their two young children, Jacqui and Jerry Jr. were sitting. "When I caught that ball, so much pressure left my body. I was very emotional.

"Jim Brown, I feel, was the greatest player of all time. No one ever thought a receiver would break this record because we don't get our hands on the ball as often as a running back does."

Brown, who is an extremely proud man and not given to easy

compliments, was unstinting in his praise of Jerry's feat.

"I love what he's doing, playing at a great level and helping the 49ers win. I admire him, and I hope he scores 100 more touchdowns. He has what a lot of players don't have, a refusal to go down and a determination to get into the end zone. He's a fighter out there."

That game set the tone for another spectacular season for Jerry, who was named the NFC Offensive Player of the Week for his work against the Raiders. Jerry also won the honor later in the season when he roped in 16 receptions for 165 yards and a trio of touchdowns against the Rams. The third of those TD's was the 56th on which Jerry had teamed up with Steve Young, one more than Joe Montana and Jerry had connected on in their storied time together. It was also in that game that Jerry became the only player in NFL history to exceed 1,000 receiving yards in nine different seasons.

Jerry finished the season with a career-high 112 receptions, 15 touchdowns, and an NFL-best 1,499 receiving yards. His performance produced a sense of awe in former teammate Dwight Clark, who now works in the front office for the 49ers. "He's been at it for 10 years, and he's better now than he was at the beginning."

Jerry's exploits, more importantly, helped the 49ers to a league-best 13–3 record, putting them in prime position for a run at the Super Bowl. Jerry actually had a quiet game in the Niners' divisional playoff-game win over the Bears. And he also put up small stats when the 49ers, who had dropped two straight NFC Championship games to the Cowboys, finally turned the tables on the team from Big D. But Jerry did team up with Steve Young on a 28-yard touchdown pass that proved to be the biggest play of the day.

After a four year absence, the 49ers had made it back to the Super Bowl, and right before the kickoff Jerry gathered his teammates around him to remind them just how important it was for them to stay focused on beating the San Diego Chargers. "This is what we've worked for, and we've come too far to let it get away."

Then Jerry went out and put on a spectacular show by catching 10 passes for 149 yards and three touchdowns.

"With all the great receivers, you know they could catch the ball," noted San Diego general manager Pete Bethard, who has been an NFL talent scout for three decades. "But with him, every time he catches it, there's a good chance he could end up scoring. That is remarkable. "There just hasn't been anybody like him."

12 No Questions, No Regrets

After only 10 seasons in the league, Jerry is well on his way to achieving—and even surpassing—all of the statistical goals that he set earlier in his career. Jerry is already the game's all-time touchdown scoring leader, while ranking second in receiving yards and 100-yard games. And he currently ranks number three in career receptions, while owning a host of regular season, postseason, and Super Bowl records.

"I really don't want to reflect on what I've done. Right now, I don't have the time. After my career is over, that's when I'll sit down and let it soak in and maybe say, 'Wow, I can't believe I broke so many records,'" said Jerry. He is so durable that he has never missed a game in his entire career, and he is so consistent that he has caught at least one pass in his last 143 games, the fourth longest streak in NFL history.

"I feel better now than when I first came into the league. I think I'm just at the peak of my football career, and I'm going to continue to work as hard as I can to be as good as I can, because I really don't want any questions after my career is over. No questions. No regrets. So when I'm on the field, it's all out every play."

But on or off the field, Jerry brings a special grace along with him. Jerry, for instance, will never spike a ball or taunt a defender. "They pay me to catch the football and make things happen," Rice says, flatly. "Once you score a touchdown, that defensive back knows you have him under control. I'm not going to spin the ball on the ground if I catch a touchdown pass. I did my job, and it's over. That's it. That's all."

When Jerry is off the field, he spends most of his time with his wife and children. "I can't wait to get home and play with the kids," says Jerry with a big smile on his face.

Jerry also spends a good deal of time talking to other people's children, something that he prepared for by taking speech lessons to polish his grammar and improve his public speaking ability.

"I needed somebody to smooth out my speech. The first time I tried to give a talk I was scared to death. I never throught I'd ever get to the point of enjoying it. But I'm comfortable with it now, and I really like getting up in front of people. It's a way that I can share what I'm doing with people.

"I try to share my enthusiasm with kids whenever I can," adds Jerry, "I sign autographs for every kid who asks and, after each season ends, I talk to teens at various high schools."

In Jerry's talks he points out the importance of training for life, and of staying away from the wrong crowd, and the danger of smoking, drinking, or taking drugs. Jerry also advises young people not to become couch potatoes and waste time watching television when they could be studying or pursuing their athletic or artistic talents.

As far as Steve Young is concerned, Jerry should be doing a lot more talking. "I wish Jerry would be more vocal about who he is because he's such a great role model for America. He could make a difference to the youth of today because of his work ethic and his intensity and his drive to be a great player. He's got humility, he has a package that brings an amazingly unique combination. I wish we could hold him up higher than he already is because he's the epitome of what I'd like young people in America to be. I would wish that every kid would say, 'I want to be a Jerry Rice.' The world would be a much better place."

Jerry is also doing his part to help to make the world a better place through the "127 Foundation," which he created with his agent, Jim Steiner.

"The foundation was created to spread money around to lots of charities. It was something we wanted to do a long time ago. But I feel now that I have a name out there, that when people hear that name, they're going to contribute to the foundation. I feel it's time now to give something to the community."

If you want to write to the author, address your letter to:

> Richard J. Brenner
> c/o East End Publishing
> 54 Alexander Dr.
> Syosset, NY 11791

Please note that letters *will not* be answered unless they include a self-addressed and stamped envelope.

If you want to write to Steve Young or Jerry Rice address your letter to:

> Steve Young (Jerry Rice)
> c/o San Francisco 49ers
> 4949 Centennial Blvd.
> Santa Clara, CA 95054

Sources

Desert News

Fantastic Flyer Magazine

Football Digest

Inside Sports

Sacramento Bee

The Salt Lake City Tribune

San Francisco Chronicle

San Francisco Examiner

San Jose Mercury

Sports Illustrated

Sport Magazine

The Sporting News

STEVEN YOUNG
Birthdate: October 11, 1961
Birthplace: Salt Lake City, Utah
Height: 6 ft. 2 in.   Weight: 200 lbs.

COLLEGE STATS

	PASSING							RUSHING			
	ATT.	COMP.	YDS.	PCT.	TD	INT.	RATING	ATT.	YDS.	AVG.	TD
1981	112	56	731	50.0	5	5	111.6	53	233	4.4	0
1982	367	233	3100	62.7	18	18	140.0	144	407	2.8	10
1983	429	306	3902	71.3	33	10	168.5	102	144	1.4	8
Totals	908	595	7733	65.5	56	33	149.9	299	784	2.6	18

REGULAR SEASON STATS

	PASSING							RUSHING			
	ATT.	COMP.	YDS.	PCT.	TD	INT.	RATING	ATT.	YDS.	AVG.	TD
1984(USFL)	310	179	2361	57.7	10	9	80.6	79	515	6.5	7
1985	250	137	1741	54.8	6	13	63.1	56	368	6.6	2
1985(TB)	138	72	935	52..2	3	8	56.9	40	233	5.8	1
1986	363	195	2282	53.7	8	14	65.5	74	425	3.5	5
1987(SF)	69	37	570	53.6	10	0	120.8	26	190	7.3	1
1988	101	54	680	53.5	3	3	72.2	27	184	6.8	1
1989	92	64	1001	69.6	8	3	120.8	38	126	3.3	2
1990	62	38	427	61.3	2	0	92.6	15	159	10.6	0
1991	279	180	2517	64.5	17	8	101.8	66	415	6.3	4
1992	402	268	3465	66.7	25	7	107.0	16	106	6.6	1
1993	462	314	4023	68.0	29	16	101.5	69	407	5.9	2
1994	461	324	3969	70.3	35	10	112.8	58	293	5.1	7
Totals	2989	1862	23971	62.3	156	91	96.8	564	3421	6.1	33

POSTSEASON STATS

	PASSING							RUSHING			
	ATT.	COMP.	YDS.	PCT.	TD	INT.	RATING	ATT.	YDS.	AVG.	TD
1984(USFL)	67	30	421	44.8	1	4	46.0	9	68	7.6	0
1987(SF)	17	12	158	70.6	1	1	94.7	6	72	12.0	1
1988	1	1	-1	10.0	0	0	79.2	3	1	0.3	0
1989	5	3	26	60.0	0	0	73.8	5	5	1.0	0
1990	1	1	25	10.0	0	0	118.8	0	0	0.0	0
1992	65	45	540	69.2	3	3	90.5	16	106	6.6	1
1993	67	44	513	65.7	1	1	87.5	10	55	5.5	1
1994	87	53	623	60.9	9	0	117.2	20	128	6.4	2
Totals	314	189	2315	60.2	15	9	99.5	69	435	6.3	5

JERRY RICE

Birthdate: October 13, 1962
Birthplace: Starkville, MS
Height: 6 ft. 2 in.   Weight: 200 lbs.

COLLEGE STATS

	NO.	YDS.	AVG.	TD
1981	30	428	14.3	2
1982	36	1,133	17.3	7
1983	102	1,450	14.2	14
1984	112	1,845	16.5	28
Totals	310	4,856	15.7	51

REGULAR SEASON STATS

| | Receiving | | | | | Rushing | | | | |
	NO.	YDS.	AVG.	LONG	TD	ATT.	YDS.	AVG.	LONG	TD
1985	49	927	18.9	66t	3	6	26	4.3	15T	1
1986	86	1570	18.3	66t	15	10	72	7.2	18	1
1987	65	1078	16.6	57t	22	8	51	6.4	17	1
1988	64	1306	20.4	96t	9	13	107	8.2	29	1
1989	82	1483	18.1	68t	17	5	33	6.6	17	0
1990	100	1502	15.0	64t	13	2	0	0.0	0	0
1991	80	1206	15.1	73t	14	1	2	2.0	2	0
1992	84	1201	14.3	80t	10	9	58	6.4	26t	1
1993	98	1503	15.3	80t	15	3	69	23.0	43t	1
1994	112	1499	13.4	69t	13	7	93	13.3	28t	2
Totals	820	13275	16.2	96t	131	64	511	8.0	43t	8

POSTSEASON STATS

| | Receiving | | | | | Rushing | | | | |
	NO.	YDS.	AVG.	LONG	TD	ATT.	YDS.	AVG.	LONG	TD
1985	4	45	11.3	20	0	0	0	0.0	0	0
1986	3	48	16.0	24	0	0	0	0.0	0	0
1987	3	28	9.3	13	0	0	0	0.0	0	0
1988	21	409	19.4	61t	6	3	29	9.6	21	0
1989	19	317	16.7	72t	5	0	0	0.0	0	0
1990	11	122	11.1	19	1	0	0	0.0	0	0
1992	14	211	15.1	36	1	1	9	9.0	9	0
1993	9	126	14.0	23	0	1	(-9)	(-9.0)	(-9)	0
1994	16	233	14.6	44t	4	1	10	10.0	10	0
Totals	100	1539	15.4	72t	17	6	39	6.5	21	0

If you enjoyed this book, you might want to order some of our other exciting titles:

BASKETBALL SUPERSTARS ALBUM 1996, Richard J. Brenner. Includes 16 full-color pages, and mini-bios of the game's top superstars, plus career and all-time stats. 48 pages.

MICHAEL JORDAN * MAGIC JOHNSON, by Richard J. Brenner. A dual biography of two of the greatest superstars of all time. 128 pages, 15 dynamite photos.

ANFERNEE HARDAWAY * GRANT HILL, by Brian Cazeneuve. A dual biography of two of the brightest young stars in basketball. 96 pages, 10 pages of photos.

SHAQUILLE O'NEAL * LARRY JOHNSON, by Richard J. Brenner. A dual biography of two of the brightest young stars in basketball. 96 pages, 10 pages of photos.

STEVE YOUNG * JERRY RICE, by Richard J. Brenner. A dual biography of the two superstars who led the 49ers to the Super Bowl. 96 pages. 10 pages of photos.

TROY AIKMAN * STEVE YOUNG, by Richard J. Brenner. A dual biography of the top two quarterbacks in the NFL. 96 pages, 10 pages of photos.

KEN GRIFFEY JR. * FRANK THOMAS, by Brian Cazeneuve. A dual biography of baseball's brightest young superstars. 96 pages, 10 pages of photos.

BARRY BONDS * ROBERTO ALOMAR, by Bob Woods. A dual biography of two of the brightest stars in baseball. 96 pages, 10 pages of photos.

MARIO LEMIEUX, by Richard J. Brenner. An exciting biography of one of hockey's all-time greats. 96 pages, 10 pages of photos.

THE WORLD SERIES, THE GREAT CONTESTS, by Richard J. Brenner. The special excitement of the Fall Classic is brought to life through seven of the most thrilling Series ever played, including 1993. 176 pages, including 16 action-packed photos.

THE COMPLETE SUPER BOWL STORY, GAMES I-XXVIII, by Richard J. Brenner. The most spectacular moments in Super Bowl history are brought to life, game by game. 224 pages, including 16 memorable photos.

MICHAEL JORDAN, by Richard J. Brenner. an easy-to-read, photo-filled biography especially for youngest readers. 32 pages.

SHAQUILLE O'NEAL, by Richard J. Brenner. An easy-to-read, photo-filled biography especially for younger readers. 32 pages.

WAYNE GRETZKY, by Richard J. Brenner. An easy-to-read, photo-filled biography especially for younger readers. 32 pages.

TOUCHDOWN! THE FOOTBALL FUN BOOK, by Richard J. Brenner. Trivia, puzzles, mazes and much more! 64 pages.

PLEASE SEE NEXT PAGE FOR ORDER FORM

ORDER FORM

Payment must accompany all orders and must be in U.S. dollars. Postage and handling is $1.35 per book up to a maximum of $6.75 ($1.75 to a maximum in Canada).

Please send me the following books:

No. of copies	Title	Price
_____	BASKETBALL SUPERSTARS ALBUM 1996	$4.50/$6.25 Can.
_____	MICHAEL JORDAN * MAGIC JOHNSON	$3.50/$4.25 Can.
_____	ANFERNEE HARDAWAY * GRANT HILL	$3.99/$5.50 Can.
_____	SHAQUILLE O'NEAL * LARRY JOHNSON	$3.50/$4.50 Can.
_____	STEVE YOUNG * JERRY RICE	$3.99/$5.50 Can.
_____	TROY AIKMAN * STEVE YOUNG	$3.50/$4.50 Can.
_____	KEN GRIFFEY JR. * FRANK THOMAS	$3.50/$4.50 Can.
_____	BARRY BONDS * ROBERTO ALOMAR	$3.50/$4.50 Can.
_____	MARIO LEMIEUX	$3.50/$4.50 Can.
_____	THE WORLD SERIES, THE GREAT CONTESTS	$3.50/$4.50 Can.
_____	THE COMPLETE SUPER BOWL STORY GAMES I-XXVIII	$4.00/$5.00 Can.
_____	MICHAEL JORDAN	$4.00/$5.50 Can.
_____	SHAQUILLE O'NEAL	$3.25/$4.50 Can.
_____	WAYNE GRETZKY	$3.25/$4.50 Can.
_____	TOUCHDOWN! THE FOOTBALL FUN BOOK	$3.50/$5.00 Can.

TOTAL NUMBER OF BOOKS ORDERED _____

TOTAL PRICE OF BOOKS $_____

POSTAGE AND HANDLING $_____

TOTAL PAYMENT ENCLOSED $_____

NAME _____

ADDRESS _____

CITY _____ STATE _____ ZIP _____ COUNTRY _____

Send to: East End Publishing, 54 Alexander Drive, Syosset NY 11791 USA. Dept. TD. Allow three weeks for delivery. Discounts are available on orders of 25 or more copies. For details call (516) 364-6383.